SINGLE DAD PARENTING LIKE A PRO

A SURVIVAL GUIDE FOR SINGLE FATHERS WITH KIDS

ALFIE THOMAS

Copyright © 2022 by Alfie Thomas. All rights reserved. Printed in the United States of America. No part of this book may be used or reproduced in any manner whatsoever without written permission except in the case of brief quotations.

Copyright © 2022 by Alfie Thomas

All rights reserved. No part of this publication may be reproduced, distributed or transmitted in any form or by any means, including photocopying, recording or any other electronic or mechanical methods, without the prior written permission of the publisher, except in the case of brief quotations embodied in critical reviews and certain other noncommercial uses permitted by copyright law.

Although the publisher and the author have made every effort to ensure that the information in this book was correct at press time and while this publication is designed to provide accurate information in regard to the subject matter overall, the publisher and author assume no responsibility for errors, inaccuracies, omissions or any other inconsistencies herein and hereby disclaim any liability to any party for any loss, damage or disruption caused by errors or omission, whether such errors or omissions result from negligence, accident or any other cause.

This publication is meant as a source of valuable information for the reader, however, it is not meant as a substitute for direct expertise assistance. If such a level of assistance is required, the services of a competent professional should be sought.

"Being a single parent is twice the work, twice the stress, and twice the tears. But also twice the hugs, twice the love, and twice the pride!"

— UNKNOWN

CONTENTS

It Was Not Supposed to be This Way   11

1. BEING A SINGLE DAD   15
   The Challenges of Being a Single Father   16
   Expectations vs Goals   20
   What is the Single Dad Mindset?   25
   Self-reflection and Introspection as a Single Father   28
   Real Life Experiences of Single Fathers   47

2. HELPING YOUR KIDS COPE WITH LOSS   51
   Divorce   53
   Absenteeism   61
   Death   69
   Strategies to Remember for any Type of Loss   76

3. SINGLE-DAD GUIDE TO TIME MANAGEMENT AND ORGANIZATION   83
   Managing Your Time   85
   Household Organization   92
   Use Technology to Your Advantage   94
   Real life Experiences of Single Fathers   96

4. SINGLE-DAD GUIDE TO MANAGING FAMILY FINANCES   99
   Financial Difficulties as a Single Father   100
   How to Manage Financial Difficulties   101
   How to Earn Extra Money as a Single Father   106
   Tips for Coping with Financial Stress   107

Applying your Skills	108
Real Life Experiences of Single Fathers	110

5. BEING A SINGLE DAD TO A DAUGHTER — 113

The Hardest Part	114
Overcome the Challenges of Raising Your Daughter	116
Doing Your Best	120
Real Life Experiences of Single Fathers	123

6. BEING A SINGLE DAD TO A SON — 127

Your Importance as a Single Father	128
Raising a Son	131
Healthy and Positive Activities for You and Your Son	138
Real Life Experiences of Single Fathers	139

7. BEING A SOLO PARENT TO A CHILD WITH SPECIAL NEEDS — 141

The Challenges	142
Survival Tips	144
Real Life Experiences of Single Fathers	148

8. THE RIGHT WAY TO DISCIPLINE CHILDREN AS A SINGLE DAD — 151

What Kind of Father are You?	152
What Not to Do	155
Disciplining Mistakes Divorced Parents Make	156
What to Do	158
Age by Age Guide	160
Get Those Chores Done	163
Real Life Experiences of Single Fathers	164

9. A NEW MOM FOR THE KIDS? — 167

Dating	168
How to Have the Dating Conversation With Your Child	171

Get Going	173
Real Life Experiences of Single Fathers	174
10. STRATEGIES FOR THE TOUGH TIMES	177
On the Verge of a Breakdown?	178
Depression & Loneliness in Single Fathers	181
Mindfulness	183
Real Life Experiences from Single Fathers	186
You are a Superhero!	189
Bibliography	193

For Mirabelle, Mercy, Ava, and Mia

IT WAS NOT SUPPOSED TO BE THIS WAY

Single fatherhood will either leave you a broken man in everyone's eyes or mold you into the ultimate hero in your children's eyes.

When my brother, Darnell, lost his wife of 15 years to Covid19, it was devastating for him and his two children. Life took a sudden turn for them. Darnell, Dominique, and Darius (his daughter and son) were left suspended in midair—lost, confused, and upset. Darnell seemed like a broken man.

I was a witness to their struggle and loss, and my heart went out to them. It was difficult for him to manage work, school, the household chores, raising children, and his social life. It was a juggling act for him which he could not get right. Moreover, Dominique was going through bodily and hormonal changes at the age of 13, and Darius, 11, was always glued to the TV or his mobile phone. Both children missed their mother tremendously and did not how to channel it.

There were many nights Darnell, feeling anxious, overwhelmed, and depressed, would call me. The help Mirabelle and I could offer to Darnell was different from having a partner. While I was there for Darnell to help and hear and support, his struggle was one that he had to internally process. Moved by Darnell's loss, I began to do research and speak to other single fathers to better understand their struggles and challenges and how they overcame them. It took me two years to gather all the information, knowledge, and analysis along with an added year to compile this book for you!

I am here and ready to help you walk through your difficult times and help you manage your life better. While life as a single father is daunting and challenging, I believe you can overcome and even flourish among the chaos and struggles to be at peace and happy with your family. You can provide the best for your children and for yourself after the loss of a partner, separation, or divorce.

By the end of the book you will be able to do the following:

- Manage your life with more semblance.
- Obtain a deeper awareness of what it is like to be single father.
- Overcome every day and long-term struggles.
- Organize your home.
- Manage finances better.
- Become more confident in assessing your child's needs.
- Discipline your children with science-backed methods.
- Learn child rearing techniques.
- Raise your children with love, care, and patience.
- Practice self-care and self-love.
- Be able to enjoy a romantic relationship without neglecting your children.
- Learn easy but powerful techniques for managing and overcoming daily stress.

Know that you are not alone on this journey. There are so many more people in the world who can understand your pain and your struggle. Even celebrities have the same challenges.

Take Idris Elba. He is a single dad and says that with his acting career alongside fathering, it gets hard, but he believes it is an important part of his life. He works hard to guide and help his children to the best of his abilities. Then there is P. Diddy, a single father to five children, who manages to spend quality time with each of them—from going to the gym with his son, to cuddling and dancing with his other children.

While celebrities do have the finances and resources which make it easier as a single father, remember that the effort comes from within your heart. Internal strength and resolve are what you need to begin. As Maya Angelou said, "If you can't change it, change your attitude." That is the key—changing your mindset and adapting.

Your life may seem in upheaval now, and I understand why. I empathize with you. However, after I witnessed Darnell turn his life around, when I saw the happiness return to his eyes, when he realized he could become the dependable and nurturing parent to his children with peace of mind and healthy stress management, I understood that I needed to share my knowledge and experiences of single fathers out there to help you achieve the same. I believe in you and your capability. You've got this!

1

BEING A SINGLE DAD

I hear you! Single parenting is not easy. I witnessed Darnell's pain firsthand. A few months after Darnell's wife, Emma, passed away, the reality of life set in. Mirabelle and I went to his house with food for him and the children, and when we got there, my heart broke.

The house was a mess. The children were already sitting in front of the TV, eating McDonald's, while Darnell was nowhere to be found. Mirabelle got to work with the children, and I went to look for Darnell. I found him in his room, sitting in Emma's favorite armchair, sobbing softly. It broke my heart. Being the younger brother, I always looked to Darnell for strength and confidence, but now he needed all the strength and comfort his younger brother could give to him. I went to him and hugged him. I told Darnell that Mirabelle and I were going to support him and be there for him whenever he needed us. I reminded him of the extended support system and that he needed to process his grief.

We had dinner together that night, and both of us had a heart to heart. I told him that while grieving is a natural process and the pain will remain, you must also consider your children's well-being. That helped Darnell take some decisive actions in his life.

From then on, I noticed how Darnell slowly began to incorporate small changes in his life and how those changes began making a difference. I joined a support group for single fathers with him, began reaching out to single fathers online, and started to read extensively on this topic. I gave my input and assistance whenever he required it.

THE CHALLENGES OF BEING A SINGLE FATHER

Statistically, your role as a single father has evolved. You are now a part of a wider community which has its fair share of challenges. Did you know that, in 2017, it was reported that 25% of US households were led by a single parent. In 2019, around 2.45 million children between the ages of 1 to 7 were living with a single parent, and out of this number, 15.17% were living with their father. Moreover, in 2017, within the 35% of cohabiting unmarried parents, 17% are single fathers (Zuckerman, 2020). According to research (Bureau, n.d.), it was stated that out of the two million single fathers, 40% were divorced, 38% were not married, 16% were separated, and 6% were widowers.

Many new single fathers are simply trying to figure out where to begin. While you are trying to adjust to change, be mindful that your child is adjusting to change as well. Yes, single parenting is tough no matter what situation you may find yourself in. However, raising children as a single father has its own share of issues. The percentage of single fatherhood has increased since the 1960s and is continuing to see an upward trend. Some of the challenges single fathers face are:

- having a conversation with your child about a parent's death or divorce
- finding support
- neglecting self-care
- organizing
- romance, love, and dating issues
- others' opinions
- fear of vulnerability

- the legal system
- financial issues
- day to day practicalities
- co-parenting
- the emotional impact of separation, divorce, or death

How can you transition effectively into your new role as a single dad? Well, it is a lot to take in. It is a change of environment, physical absence of your partner, financial fluctuations, emotions and feelings, and added responsibility. Just listing these spotlights just how much is going on at one time!

However, we humans are made to adapt and to mold ourselves according to the changes we go through in our life. Changes will be tough; there is no debating that fact. I want you to be aware of the changes, so you do not feel you have been thrown into a deep abyss. When Darnell lost his wife to an illness, it was unexpected. He had no idea what to do, and seeing him struggle with the changes and his new reality was extremely upsetting for me. We do not have control over life and death; however, if you are separating or divorcing, you need to know the changes you will be faced with. There will most definitely be changes that you will be happy with and others that you will not be.

There are some advantages working in favor of single dads. For example, single fathers are more likely to live with a cohabiting partner according to research conducted by Pew in 2013 (The Rise of Single Fathers, 2013). Hence, they are not always alone. In regards to income, education, and poverty, single fathers are better off than single mothers according to a study done on the aforementioned research. (Single-Father Families: A Review of the Literature, 2015).

Yes, these are motivating and uplifting facts; however, it does not take away from the fact that there are still challenges for you as a single father. Moreover, the stereotype that men are not good caretakers does us no favors either. People will doubt your capability, your parenting skills, and your ability to be a good parent, just because you are a man. Because men can be unfortunately conditioned with implicit messages of "be strong," "your only responsibility is finances," "you should never cry," and "anger is the only emotion," they think it their nature to behave this way. Nobody is born being a caregiver or a nurturing human. We learn these traits. The fact that society pushes gender-specific roles makes it even tougher to break free of the stereotypes.

I am here to tell you that you have it in you to be nurturing, loving, caring, and gentle. As men, we are capable of all those emotions. You are capable of bonding with your family and setting a healthy precedent. There are various issues to be mindful of as a single father. Just remember, be honest, open, and communicate. These changes can go a long way in your relationship with your child. Your child considers you their role model, so you are setting a great example by making these small shifts and changes here and there.

EXPECTATIONS VS GOALS

As we all know, society has gender stereotypes which confine us, damage our perceptions, and stifle our growth. Luckily, we are now moving toward doing away with many of those stereotypes, but some still exist when it comes to parenting. There are certain mother duties and certain father duties. Darnell and his wife were like two cogs in a wheel. They worked well together and did not adhere to stereotypes of the man being the breadwinner and the woman doing everything else.

It is all about dividing the workload, not the roles, in a marriage. Unfortunately, the bar set for fathers is very low; they can get away with doing next to nothing. For instance, if a father is staying home to take care of their child while the wife is busy with work, it is applauded, praised, and commented on. If the roles are reversed, however, there is rarely a single peep of appreciation because that is the "woman's duty."

When you become a single father, these expectations and stereotypes can be damaging because they make you feel incapable of all the things your ex-partner would do. A single father may struggle with the most basic task. Along with expecting the bare minimum, society will often question whether you are fit enough to rear a child alone. We must choose to ignore these expectations and set reachable, realistic goals. Let us look at a few examples of how expectations and goals should be realigned.

Waking Your Children

- **Expectation for the mother:** Kiss your children, tiptoe into their room, and wake them up to a song. Have a healthy breakfast waiting on the table.
- **Expectation for the father:** The children will wake up to the alarm. Call out to them and give them a bowl of cereal for breakfast.
- **Goal:** Wake your child up in a consistent manner. Decide what they will have for breakfast beforehand.

Academics and School

- **Expectation for the mother**: Oversee the class group, attend all parent teacher meetings, volunteer as a chaperone to class outings, bake delicious brownies for the bake sale, drop and pick them from school, and help with their homework. And this must be done with a smile on your face while looking like a super model.
- **Expectation for the father:** Drop off your children to school when you have time in the morning. Know your child's teacher's name and email in case of an emergency.
- **Goal:** Drop off and pick up your child and have a carpool system as well. Ask them if they need help with their homework. When extra work needs to be done regarding school, know it beforehand, so you have ample time to ask for help or prepare.

Your Child's Friends

- **Expectation for the mother:** Know each friend by name. Know their allergies, likes, and dislikes. Plan play dates, keep in touch with the friend's parents, and plan social activities with them.

- **Expectation for the father:** Who is who? Is Samantha the tall one or the one with braces?
- **Goal:** Make a group on WhatsApp (or another group messaging service) with your their friends' parents and ask your child about who they play with and like to hang out with in school.

Doing the Laundry

- **Expectation for the mother:** Have all the laundry sorted. See to the whites and colors. Make sure there is fabric softener, iron the clothes, fold them neatly, and put them in respective family members' closets.
- **Expectation for the father:** Pick up the clothes and throw them into the washing machine (no separating whites and colors), put them in the dryer, and leave them there.
- **Goal:** Do laundry on a Friday night and leave the ironing for a Saturday. (Of course, these could be different days that work best.) This way, you won't be too tired from washing, drying, ironing, and folding on the same day.

Household Chores

- **Expectation for the mother:** Keep the house sparkling and neat by vacuuming, dusting, washing dishes, and organizing.
- **Expectation for the father:** Doesn't the house look alright the way it is? (While, in reality, the house is a mess).
- **Goal:** Clean over the weekend. If your children are old enough, ask them to help you with household chores. If you can afford it, hire help to come in and clean once a week.

Manners

- **Expectation for the mother:** Stay in the loop of your child's life, teaching them the basics of social etiquettes and disciplining them. You are the "bad cop" and resident therapist.
- **Expectation for the father:** It is ok to say swear words in front of them and tell them to fight back if anyone ever tries to bully them.
- **Goal:** Stay active in disciplining your child and keep communication open.

Feeding Children

- **Expectation for the mother:** Google healthy and fun meal plans. Watch YouTube tutorials on how to pack school lunches in a creative way and buy only organic ingredients for healthy meals.
- **Expectation for the father:** Who wants to order pizza?
- **Goal:** Prepare meals and lunchboxes in advance. Do not make food that will rot faster.

These are only a few examples of the stark difference in expectations of a mother and a father. But it is time to change that. Take control of your life. Disregard stereotypes, and once you see what you are capable of, you will be unstoppable!

WHAT IS THE SINGLE DAD MINDSET?

Apart from the physical and financial changes, you will also have to change your mindset when adjusting to your new role. Changing a mindset requires time, effort, and patience. Learning may be easy, but unlearning is more difficult. Now that you are a single father, a lot has changed. Remind yourself of these important things as you begin your journey:

- **You can do this!** Yes, it is a new and mysterious territory. There will be fear. How will you navigate? What will you do? Are you doing the right thing? Tell yourself that you can do it. Sit with the feeling of fear, acknowledge you are scared, and figure out what you fear. When you understand your fear and begin to untangle it, you will erode the crippling fear and begin to believe thoughts like, *I have got this, I can do this, and I am doing a good enough job.*
- **Step into the single father duties and process quickly.** To clarify, I do not mean dive right into everything the day after you get divorced or a day after you have lost your partner. Give yourself time to process and grieve. However, do not let the enormity of your task get to you. You cannot let it stop you from taking on the new role of a single father. The more you feed your fear, the more it will take control of your thoughts. Get into the responsibilities and duties once you feel you are ready.
- **Be empathic and sympathetic.** Offer empathy and sympathy to not just your children but yourself as well. Please build this into your new single father mindset. This is just the beginning, and along the way, you will face all sorts of new challenges. So, please offer patience and

empathy to yourself and your children. It will go a long way.

- **Manage your expectations and do not avoid your feelings.** You will feel all sorts of emotions: anger, hurt, anxiety, and stress. Moreover, you may think you can manage everything alone, but be realistic. Instead, remind yourself that you can manage everything in your own time, but it does not need to be perfect—just good enough. Keep your expectations realistic, not idealistic. Moreover, when you do feel any emotion, do not let it go unchecked for it to boil over later. Because that will most likely happen. Your environment will be a stressor with so many new changes; there will be a lot going on. So, acknowledge feelings and process them in your time, rather than bottling them and bursting open at the slightest of triggers.
- **Keep everything in perspective.** Rather than falling into a self-pitying mindset and wondering *why did this happen to me* and *how will I ever manage?* Remind yourself that you are capable and can, in fact, manage. Look, I know it is difficult, and things will be up and down over the course of your single father journey, but it is possible. There will be days when you

feel you cannot do it anymore. On those days, remind yourself of how far you have already come.

- **Your happiness depends on you—nobody else.** While your children are an extremely important part of your life, and they will make you happy, it is not their job to do so. Your happiness is yours. Do not solely work toward making your child happy by doing everything they want. Instead, work toward giving them a consistent and safe environment. But remember your happiness will come from within.

So, get right into it and start working on adjusting your mindset!

SELF-REFLECTION AND INTROSPECTION AS A SINGLE FATHER

Our brain is always functioning, always putting together bits and pieces, making sense, observing, and so on. However, amidst all this critical thinking we forget to apply basic concepts to ourselves.

What exactly is introspection? It is diving into your thoughts, emotions, and feelings. It is looking within to see what is going on. Ask yourself, do you ever slow down to introspect, to take a breath, or to pause? It is not easy; we are so caught up in daily life that we forget to just slow down and be in the here and now.

Let's be honest, it is a rat race out there. Everyone is constantly on the go, wanting to achieve the next goal, reach the next target, and just keep striving for what is next. If that works for you, go for it, but remember, it is not the healthiest way to live. So, I suggest you take out some time in the day, even if it is 10 minutes, to just sit down by yourself and have a look within. This could be 10 minutes of silence or even journaling. It will seem odd at first if it is something completely new for you, but you will get used to it. Please make it a habit. Following are ways in which introspection can be a positive aspect in your life:

- **You will notice any negative patterns in your life.** You may be in an unhealthy pattern or cycle in your life. It could be overworking yourself, doing too much for others or being in a toxic relationship. When you sit down to introspect, you will be able to observe these patterns. Learn your triggers and how these triggers affect you in terms of feelings and emotions. Then, you can figure out how to step away from the toxic patterns and find a better alternative that makes you happy rather than leave you mentally and physically drained.

- **You will focus on the bigger picture.** When we are caught up in everyday life, we sometimes lose sight of what our goal in life is. And then, you will hit a low and wonder *why am I doing all of this?* and *what is the point in this?* So, sit down with yourself and remember why you are doing what you are doing. You can write it down, say it aloud to yourself, and remind yourself time to time. Once you acknowledge your goal frequently, daily tasks will not seem as monotonous and frustrating.
- **You will stop worrying about things that are not in your control.** Things that are out of your control—anything in the external environment—are not worth worrying over. No matter how much you plan your life, there will be some elements that you will not have control over. This might stress you out, frustrate you, or even anger you, but remind yourself that you do not have a choice in controlling everything, but you do have a choice in how you react to it! Instead of wasting your negative mental energy toward an event beyond your control, you can channel it inward to improve how you think and feel.

- **You will be better able to face your fears.** We all have fears. If someone says they are not fearful of anything, it is not true. It could be the fear of failure, fear of rejection, fear of abandonment, and so on. When you make the space for yourself to sit and think, you will be better able to admit what your fear is and figure out how to overcome it. While acknowledging your fear will be scary, it is the first step toward a healthier thought process which will benefit you.
- **You can set your own terms of happiness.** When do you feel the happiest? What sparks joy within you? When do you feel most proud of yourself? Ask yourself these questions, and as cliché as they sound, they will be effective at helping you figure out where your happiness lies. When you acknowledge what makes you happy and proud and make more time for those things, you will initiate a healthy cycle for yourself.
- **You can make decisions based on your conscience.** As mentioned before, people in your life will have all sorts of opinions on everything pertaining to you. Rather than taking in the opinions you do not agree with or getting annoyed at what they have to say,

introspect to really figure out your needs and your comfort. Make your choices based on what you want, not what others want. Yes, you can take advice and feedback, but at the end of the day, it is your decision. With practiced introspection, you will better be able to know what you think is right for you.
- **You will see results.** When we become more mindful and aware of ourselves and understand our feelings, we can know better what we want in our life. When we are constantly on the go, our mind blocks itself from doing anything else.

These changes will require time, effort, and consistency. Working on yourself is a journey, not a destination. While changes will be scary and new, they will work well for you and your mental and physical well-being.

Now that you know the importance of introspection and self-reflection, make a single father parenting worksheet. I have included a sheet I found extremely valuable (*Parenting Worksheets (Assessment Tool)*, 2016), and many single fathers I spoke to felt the same about it. Fill it in and see how it works out for you.

Communication Worksheet

From the moment a child is born they start to communicate with those around them. One important thing in understanding your child is learning how they communicate what they need and how they feel.

Listening is the key to communication with your child. Listening means giving your full attention to what your child has to say. It also means watching their behaviour and actions because children often find it difficult to put their feelings and thoughts into words because they don't have the language. (NSPCC 1998 positive parenting)

Please circle the words that describe **what you experienced** as a child from your parents/carers.

Circle the words below...

Nagging	Anger	Honesty	Changing their mind
Encouragement	Shouting	Patience	Trusting
Teasing	Firmness	Consistency	Being laughed at
Blaming	Being too busy	Violence	Openess
Loving	Smacking	Listening	Sharing
Listening	Hugging	Being Valued	Boundaries

Try and think about the words you have circled and decide which words you would describe as **helpful** and **unhelpful** parenting.

Write the words below...

Helpful Parenting	Unhelpful Parenting

Write the words in the circles...
which you feel are the most important to you and your child from your helpful parenting list.

SHEFFIELD Safeguarding Children Board

You and your child

Before our next session
Think about the words you would like to add to the **helpful parenting list** that you use with your child.

_____
_____
_____
_____

When we act in an open and accepting way with our children and when children are respected as individuals and listened to, it affects the way they see themselves. They grow in self confidence and learn to respect their own feelings and those of others.

Emotional Development
Worksheet

This worksheet explores how you can meet your child's emotional needs.

As a child gets to know a person who creates feelings of comfort and security, a special bond develops. The more a child is cuddled and loved, the more affection you show your child, the stronger the bond is likely to be.

Have a think about how you show affection to your child and **list the words below.**

_____
_____
_____
_____
_____
_____

Write down 3 things that are wonderful about your child

1. _____
2. _____
3. _____

Now have a think about 3 things that you really enjoy about being a parent

1. _____
2. _____
3. _____

Think about a time when **someone said something nice** about your behaviour, appearance or achievements.

What was it?

_____
_____
_____

How did it feel?

_____
_____
_____

How does your child know when you give them positive attention?

_____
_____
_____

Before the next session...

think about how your child knows when you give them **positive attention**. Be careful to notice and comment when they are behaving well and make sure your child can see your face and knows by your smile and tone of voice that you are giving them praise. Remember to write down the reaction of your child when you give them your **positive attention**.

Write below...

what your child says or does when you give them **positive attention** over the next few weeks and how their response makes you feel.

_____
_____
_____
_____
_____
_____

Boundaries and Guidance Worksheet

Boundaries are the limits that you set on activities or relationships; they help to define what is acceptable or unacceptable in a relationship. Firm boundaries also help to make a child feel secure as they 'know where they stand'.

Sometimes setting **boundaries** can be difficult and there may be times when you feel like giving in. It may be useful to share this worksheet with someone close to you as they may be able to help you in this challenge.

There may be someone who helps you with childcare e.g. partner or parent. If all the people around your child are delivering the same message this will help you to maintain **boundaries**.

Remember: if there is no consistency there is no boundary.

Considering **'boundaries'**, think about your partner/sibling/friends. What are the boundaries that exist in your relationship?

Write below...

_____
_____
_____
_____
_____
_____
_____
_____
_____

Now consider...
- What action(s) would you take if these boundaries were crossed?
- If your immediate thought is 'none', consider the message this gives out.
- How will you teach your child about boundaries if you find it difficult to enforce your own?
- What impact will this have on your child?

Striking the balance

Think back to your childhood, do you remember growing up in a strict household **(rigid boundaries)** or did you grow up in a household where you were able to do as you please **(no boundaries)**?

- Were you allowed to express your feelings?
- Did you always get your own way?
- Were you always being told 'no'?
- How did this make you feel?

RIGID boundaries	**Parent has all the power.** No two way communication as parent is always right
Consequence	Can lead to child's withdrawal or rebellion

At the other extreme

NO boundaries	**Child has all the power**
Consequence	Child can run riot and feel insecure. Parent's word has no effect on child

It is essential that there is a balance. It is important that your child's thoughts and feelings are considered so that your child feels believed and listened to which in turn helps them to develop emotionally.

However, there are times when **boundaries** need to be reinforced regardless of what your child feels he/she may want/need e.g. removing a child from a dangerous situation, for example, playing on the road.

Enhancing boundaries and communication

It is important that...

	Yes	No	Not sure
My child can express his thoughts and opinions			
I give my child instructions where necessary			
I am a friend to my child			
I talk to my child about everything			
I listen to my child			

Consider if there are any exceptions to what you have marked above.

Play and Stimulation Worksheet

This worksheet looks at how you and others can meet your child's developmental needs and provide a safe, stimulating environment for your child.

Play and stimulation

What is meant by stimulation?

Play and **stimulation** are essential for a child's physical, emotional and intellectual development (learning). By thinking about how you can provide appropriate **stimulation**, you are showing that you are striving to meet you child's changing needs.

You are also showing that you are trying to get to know them as an individual by learning about their likes and dislikes. It is important that you try to make a **stimulating** environment at home.

A **stimulating** environment is one that offers something pleasant for all your child's senses (touch, smell, sight, taste and hearing)

List 3 things that you enjoyed as a young child

1.

2.

3.

Moods and under/over stimulation

Our emotional state can change throughout the day, sometimes from hour to hour. Sometimes we want to be quiet and reflect on our thoughts; during this time we may not want to talk to people.

How would you feel if someone did not respect this? How would your child feel? Other times we may feel happy, talkative or excited.

Considering your own moods, complete the exercise below.

Your mood	What helps	What doesn't help
Irritable		
Sad/tearful		
Bored		
Excited		
Tired		

List 4 activities which incorporate the following senses

Taste is not included here as it is not appropriate before 6 months of age

Smell

Touch

Hearing

Sight

Make all the activities fun, even everyday tasks like bathing, nappy changing and feeding. Just simple activities like smiling at your baby strengthens the bond between you both and helps your baby's brain develop.

Before the next session

Think about your home environment and whether this provides adequate stimulation for your child. Think about how your child will be affected if the environment is not stimulating enough for your child.

Do you have access to books or toys? If not, can you think of any places where you may be able to access them? Ask your health visitor if you are not sure.

Behaviour Worksheet

As your child grows up, their personality will start to develop and they will challenge the boundaries or routines (or both) that you have set. The following worksheet will help you look at these behaviours and how to address them.

When you were a child, can you remember what happened to you if you didn't do as you were told?

Circle the words below which represent how you might feel when you have to say 'no' to your child.

Mean   Uneasy   Happy   Not bothered   At ease

Why do you think you feel like this?

What would happen if you didn't say no?

Instead of saying 'no' are there any other courses of action you could take?

Ways to manage inappropriate behaviour

1. **Verbal reminder**
2. **Time out**
3. **Temporary loss of privilege**

Use 1 before moving onto 2 and 3. Always follow through otherwise 1 will bear no meaning whatsoever. Consequences should always reflect the severity of the inappropriate **behaviour**. Smacking and withdrawing love (e.g. ignoring the child for prolonged periods) are never acceptable ways of managing **behaviour**.

Coping with challenging behaviour

Make sure you talk to someone and try to get their help and support. This might be someone who is a family member or a friend. You may find it easier to talk to someone outside of the family e.g. health visitor, children's centre worker.

Increasing pleasant activities

You may feel at times, when you are enforcing boundaries, that you are the 'bad cop' and this may make you feel uncomfortable. When you feel like this try taking 2-5 minutes to think about the benefits of boundary setting to you and your child.

It is important to remind yourself that every parent will find this a challenge at times.

Perhaps it would help if you make sure that you and your child take part in a pleasant activity each day.

List 5 activities below that you think you would enjoy doing with your child

1.
2.
3.
4.
5.

Effects on my child and me
Worksheet

Drugs/alcohol can affect health, relationships, housing, finances and safety for you and your child.

This worksheet will help you think about what happens to you when you drink or take drugs and the impact on your child.

Think about the affect that taking drugs or alcohol has on you and your child.

	Me		My child	
	Good	Bad	Good	Bad
Health				
Relationships				
Finance				
Housing				
Safety				

Now think about how life may look for you and your child if you **stopped drinking or taking drugs**.

What good things may you see?

Health	Relationships	Safety

Finances	Housing	Routines

Which of the '**good**' things are most important to you and what is most important for your child?

Before our next session spend time reading through the list you have made.
Consider any other thoughts that you have about the affects of your substance misuse.

Stability and Support
Worksheet

This worksheet looks at how you can provide a stable environment for your child and find support networks to help you with this.

Your child needs to grow up in a **consistent and stable** environment. This will help him/her to develop and maintain a secure attachment with you as well as other important people and places around them.

Thinking back to your own childhood what were the **consistent and stable factors** in your life?

These may have been good or bad (consider house moves, friendships etc).

46 | ALFIE THOMAS

How stable/consistent are factors in your life at present?

Indicate on the scale

Relationships

Partner	Unstable (unsatisfactory)	0	1	2	3	4	5	6	7	8	9	10	Stable (Satisfactory)
Parent(s)	Unstable (unsatisfactory)	0	1	2	3	4	5	6	7	8	9	10	Stable (Satisfactory)
Family	Unstable (unsatisfactory)	0	1	2	3	4	5	6	7	8	9	10	Stable (Satisfactory)
Friends	Unstable (unsatisfactory)	0	1	2	3	4	5	6	7	8	9	10	Stable (Satisfactory)
Housing	Unstable (unsatisfactory)	0	1	2	3	4	5	6	7	8	9	10	Stable (Satisfactory)
Health	Unstable (unsatisfactory)	0	1	2	3	4	5	6	7	8	9	10	Stable (Satisfactory)
Work/Finances	Unstable (unsatisfactory)	0	1	2	3	4	5	6	7	8	9	10	Stable (Satisfactory)
Drugs/Alcohol use	Unstable (unsatisfactory)	0	1	2	3	4	5	6	7	8	9	10	Stable (Satisfactory)

Considering the scales you have just completed, how happy are you with this?
Are there improvements you could make? How would you make these changes and if things stay as they are, what does this mean to you and your child?

Making changes permanent

If you have indicated that you would like to make changes, you may need to enlist the help of others.

To do this, it might help if you jotted down your support network.

Support Network

Remember that you have come a long way and that if you need help or support just ask! Make sure you have contact details for the following people/agencies stored somewhere safely:

Health Visitor, Children's Centre, NHS Direct, Drug/Alcohol Service, Housing Office, School

REAL LIFE EXPERIENCES OF SINGLE FATHERS

When I was conducting research on single fathers, I spoke to quite a few single fathers to get a better understanding. I even interviewed some single fathers to gain insight into what life is really like for them. I want to share their wisdom with you, so you know that you are not alone in your journey.

Some of the stories are touching, some are heartfelt, and some are sad, but at the end of the day, they are all about the human experience.

"One of [the] main stresses was finances and not being able to give my children the time they would need. I lost my wife to an accident and was left alone to take care of four children. People would be shocked that I was looking after four children, but I know I would not change it for anything in the world."

-Dan A. (Oregon)

"I wanted to give my daughter the world. But I just knew that was not possible. I wanted to make her happy, but her happiness was living together as a family with her mother, my ex-wife. I knew I could not give her this happiness, and it was heartbreaking to know that no matter how much time or

affection I gave my daughter, the one thing she really truly wanted was something I could not give."

- Alex C. (Alberta, Canada)

"When I became a single father, all the fun out of fatherhood was taken away. Now I was the father who made my child do their homework, the one who laid curfews, the one who the child confided in, the one who disciplined the child. But despite all these roles I took on for my child, I knew there was nothing else I would rather do than be there for my child, no matter what."

- Derek G. (Manhattan)

"When my daughter would tell me about other mother-daughter relationships, it would break my heart. I knew her mother could not be replaced, and I felt helpless. I knew she would struggle and compare her life to her friends,' and it was so difficult for me. But I knew I was being the best possible father to her, and I knew that was all I could offer, and it had to be good enough."

- Ryan B. (Arizona)

"It gets lonely and there have been a lot of struggles. Everyone seems to be questioning your abilities, your caretaking, your

intentions, and it is just so frustrating. Everyone looks at what you are not doing as opposed to what you are actually doing. But I have learned to be happy in knowing what I am doing. As long as my child and I are happy, that is what matters most to me!"

- Paul D. (Maine)

Being a single father is challenging my friend; I am not taking that away, but you can either allow it to break you or mold you. I hope you choose the latter because you will need it and so will your children.

In the next chapter I will tackle the first crucial challenge of being a single father—reassuring and helping your child cope with divorce, separation, loss, and absence of a mother in the family.

2

HELPING YOUR KIDS COPE WITH LOSS

Darnell, my brother, lost his wife to covid19. It came as a surprise and shock to him and his family. During the first week after his wife's loss, Darnell would constantly say, "I am left on my own," and it was very upsetting to see him in that state. It was a difficult and terrible time. Not only did Darnell have to deal with his emotions but his children's as well. It was just so overwhelming and heart wrenching. And I was just an observer. He was living through it; so, I cannot even imagine how tough it must have been on him.

I think the reality set in when Darnell was done with the formalities, such as the funeral, death certificate, speaking to banks, and closing accounts. Once that was dealt with, what he needed the most was a support system and a safe space to grieve. It was such a contrast; he went from dealing with a bureaucratic nightmare into a well of depression and sadness. It was obvious that coping with everything was becoming overwhelming for Darnell.

We were there for Darnell. We asked him to allow himself to grieve and told him to take therapy and process everything. Slowly, he began to regain a semblance of normality and take hold of his life. He was aware he had to take on more responsibility, and so he started to make minor changes in his life. He also realized he needed to look after himself—physically and emotionally—to look after his children. During this time he told me, "Alfie, if I collapse, I know my children will too, so I have to look after my needs and happiness too." This was such a powerful statement coming from someone who was grieving his wife.

He began going to the gym more regularly, attending therapy, eating cleaner, and taking out small pockets of time for himself during the day. While he said it was a struggle balancing time, he said it was essential to do so.

Seeing Darnell rise from the throes of sorrow and depression made me realize how it is possible to do so. And if you feel you are in a similar place as my brother, please know there is light at the end of the tunnel.

DIVORCE

I do not want to scare you, but before telling you about the effects, I want to highlight that all these can be helped through positive parenting, which anyone can practice.

Effects

According to a study in *The Guardian* (Campbell & editor, 2019), parental separation is most likely to harm the mental health of children who at the time of separation are at least 7 years old. Minors aged between 7 and 14 exhibit a 16% risk in emotional problems such as anxiety and depression and an 8% increase in conduct disorders. In contrast, children whose parents separate when they are between the ages of 3 and 7 are not more likely to develop such problems—either immediately or by the age of 14.

The top five effects of divorce on children are:

1. **Uncertainty:** There is going to be uncertainty about where they fit, about their family, and about the world around them. Children get their sense of security and predictability from their home. The first three years of life are crucial developmental times for children. When this phase is disrupted due to divorce, it brings

up a lot of questions for them about how stable, secure, and safe they are in this world and the uncertainty about what is to come.

2. **Conflicting Loyalties:** Because they love both their parents, children feel pulled one way or the other when their parents are no longer together. This is the most psychologically damaging aspect of divorce on children. They think that they must choose or select one of their parents to remain loyal to, and they must dismiss the other. Sometimes, parents make this worse because they have the same mentality and try to muddy the other parent's name. This is not healthy, and this puts children in a difficult position. Imagine what position it puts our children in when we tell them to declare their loyalty to one parent? It takes a lot of maturity on the parents' behalf to not embroil the child in this game, but believe me, it will help your child.

3. **Reconciliation Fantasies:** This is a psychological term referring to the fact that children tend to continue to hope, wish, or dream that their parents will get back together. Parents know that this will not happen, but children will continue to have these fantasies regardless. These thoughts are normal, and it is

helpful if parents can negotiate an arrangement that allows children to freely love each of their parents separately. Reconciliation fantasies are so strong that they show up in adults who have divorced parents as well. This typically occurs when they have not processed their grief and trauma.

4. **Alienation Syndrome:** This is also known as parental alienation syndrome, and it can be very damaging. This occurs when one parent or both poison the water a little bit and sow seeds of discontent against the other parent in the child. This is a toxic thing to do! Please honor and respect the other parent, even though it is not easy. You will require maturity for this, and you need to live with integrity.

5. **Anxiety and Depression:** Anxiety and depression are a common occurrence amongst children who have lived through divorce. When children feel threatened, unsafe, unsteady, or unable to cope with such intense feelings, they can develop anxiety. Moreover, when children start to blame themselves for the divorce or separation, it can lead to depression.

Furthermore, research states that "parental divorce/separation is associated with an increased risk for child and adolescent adjustment problems, including academic difficulties (e.g., lower grades and school dropout), disruptive behaviors (e.g., conduct and substance use problems), and depressed mood" (D'Onofrio & Emery, 2019).

Coping

Two things I would encourage you to do are to educate yourself on the effects of divorce and minimize conflict revolving around the children. If you get into a custody dispute, it will be hard on your children, and you need to be aware of that.

You see, a child's world consists of a mother and father, and they view that as their safe and happy haven where everything is contained. When parents separate, the child's world also separates. That is a new and disconcerting place for them to be. The child views his world in two different perspectives—mother's world and father's world.

How can you help your child cope with divorce and separation?

- **Believe that your child can handle it.** Children are resilient. What we believe about our children affects our behavior toward them. Hence, when we believe they can handle it, we will treat them differently than when we think they cannot. If you treat them as if they cannot manage, you will then constantly apologize to make up for what you have put them through. I know it is not easy, but you need to get past it and understand your child can handle this. They are capable because you will give them the resources they need.

- **Do not badmouth the other parent.** Do not talk negatively about your ex-partner in front of your child or even to others. You see, it changes the energy of the entire family dynamic. It changes you and gets into your mind, which can be harmful to your children. While it is important to express how you are feeling, there is a clear line between badmouthing and expressing your disappointment.
- **Do not think badly about the other parent.** This may sound like a difficult and sweeping statement. It is human to be upset and have negative thoughts. However, when you feel it is taking over your entire mind and affecting how you are treating your children, then you need to put a stop to it. I do not mean you need to repress your thoughts. Instead, process them in the correct space and manner. You need to

create a positive response for your child. When your mind is preoccupied with anger and vitriol towards your ex-partner, it affects everything you do, including your relationship with your children, work, hobbies, and even finances.

- **Focus on your job.** What is your job as a parent? Your job as a parent is to love your children. Do not get distracted thinking you have to protect them from an ex-partner or the extraneous environment. Put all that to rest and focus on your job—love your children no matter what. Imagine this from the child's perspective. The common fear is that parents will stop loving them after a divorce; after all, the parents did stop loving each other. Provide them with enough love so they know this fear dissipates.

- **Reassure you child that you will handle the tough questions.** Questions about where they will live, how much time they will spend with each parent, and where all their belongings will be are frequent questions. It is a lot of emotional burden for a child (teenagers too) to have them call the shots and be responsible for all these logistics. It is not their job. Asking a child who they want to live with can be the stressor that pushes them over the edge. Please, let's not put the burden on them, we must get past our issues as adults and reassure them that you have it under control.

- **Remember that parent issues are not child issues.** Repeat this to yourself. The issues you are worried about are not the same issues they worry or care about. It is easy to project this onto our children because we lose sight. You may be caught up in the process of thinking about how many days you have the child or what the child support arrangement will be. While your children will be thinking about how they will get to their soccer game or how they will prepare for their math test. If they are thinking about your issues instead of theirs, it is a sign that you are involving them too much in the divorce dynamic.
- **Take care of the problems in your world.** There are things going on in your ex-partner's life that you do not know much about and cannot control. Your child now lives in the shared space between you and your ex-partner. If you do not like how they are doing something and are not supportive of their ways, then you should know, you cannot do much about that. Handle the problems in your own

world where you have control. Create a sane, stable, and loving environment for your child instead. Know that it is healthy to let it go! You cannot take control in your ex-partners life, and you will create conflict if you try.

- **Stay in leveler mode.** There will be two choices: victim mode or leveler mode. If you are blaming everyone else and slipping into scarcity, that is victim mode. What do I mean by leveler mode? Well, it is the mode where you are not the victim, rescuer, or persecutor. Instead, you are thinking in a levelheaded manner for yourself and your children. This way, you can be in control of your life without having your ex-partner and circumstances dictate your life.

- **Take good care of yourself, so your children do not have to.** Children are worried about you, especially if they are old enough to understand what is going on in your life. Children will get into an awkward position when they feel they must take care of their parents. Be mindful of the fact that this is not a healthy dynamic. Please take out the time to go to therapy, exercise, keep up a social life, sleep well, and so on! This will create a positive family dynamic.

- **Practice positivity.** It is what it is! I know it is painfully hard, and these can be trying circumstances. However, no matter what is going on, remember you have the power and tell yourself you have got this! Always work with the mindset of "inside out." When things are peaceful and happy within you, it will be easier to show up for your children.
- **Stick to a routine.** We are creatures of habit; routines provide comfort. When things are slightly topsy-turvy, sticking to your child's established routine will provide them comfort.

ABSENTEEISM

How do we heal from the hurt of not having a good enough mother? It is a difficult issue to deal with. Attachment is so important for a child because it communicates to us that we have a safe foundation. It is like a safe harbor, in which we can anchor our boat.

Effects

When children have an emotionally neglectful mother, or an absent mother, it can affect children in numerous ways:

- **Regulation of Emotions:** Any emotion they feel is scary because they do not receive reassurance or were not comforted as children. Usually when a child cries, a mother or father comforts them by saying, "it is okay, don't worry." But in emotionally absent mothers, children do not hear this or experience the feeling of being comforted and soothed. Hence, when they feel any emotions, it is overwhelming for them.
- **Ability to Empathize:** Since children with absent mothers never received love and attention, they will also struggle to give it to others. They may struggle with being able to empathize with other people as well. Since they are not okay expressing themselves, they feel uncomfortable when others express their emotions.
- **Relationships:** Such children do not let people get close to them because it does not feel comfortable or safe for them. Anything that is emotionally driven makes them uncomfortable.

Hence, social relationships suffer over the course of their life. They had very little trust as children and were not taught the necessary social skills. Making connections with others may prove to be difficult. Moreover, they also have the tendency to develop a dependency on people who are caring toward them.

- **Poor Behavior:** Poor behavior shows up in the form of being unresponsive to instructions, hurting themselves, and making irrational demands. Children with absent mothers exhibit moodiness and anger.
- **Self-Image:** Children with absent mothers struggle with feelings of loneliness or worthlessness, since they were never made to feel loved or worthy of attention. This can present as signs of depression, anxiety, low self-esteem, and irritability. Moreover, these feelings can come out in the form of anger and frustration.
- **Health Issues:** When children are faced with the loss or absence of their mother, they may lose their appetite. Together with emotional stresses, this can lead to issues in the child's health.

Coping

It is a difficult situation, but believe me, you can manage. The following are ways you can help your child cope with an absent mother:

- **Be prepared.** The truth is that the mother is not around, and you cannot keep that hidden from your child no matter how much you try. Children are intuitive, and it is not a realistic scenario to keep them sheltered. Your child will ask you questions, such as:

  - Who is my mother?
  - Where is she?
  - Why is she not living with us?
  - Will she come back?
  - Can I meet her?
  - Why do my friends have mothers, and I don't?

By anticipating these questions, you can prepare yourself in a fitting manner and be ready to answer them rather than being caught off guard and completely ignoring the questions.

- **Be honest.** I know you come from a good place of wanting to protect your child from the harsh reality, but you must ask yourself if it does them any favors to conceal the truth. Before telling them, do consider their age and the situation. If your child is young, give them simple answers; however, if your child is older, then tell them accordingly. Children need to know it is not their fault, so you must be honest with them. At some point, the truth will come out. It just ends up doing more damage and will also hurt your relationship with the child if you have been dishonest.

- **Validate your child's feelings.** When your child does speak to you about how they are feeling, do not silence them, brush them off, or avoid it. Make sure you provide them with active listening. I believe active listening and validating your child's feelings will give them a sense of empathy and safety. They know they can find a safe space in you to talk about their innermost fears and emotions. Try employing phases such as: "I understand what you are feeling." "I know this is difficult for you." "It is okay to feel whatever you are feeling."
- **Lift their self-esteem.** Because children internalize everything, you must be mindful of counteracting their negative thoughts. Usually, a child will believe a parent is not around because of their doing or their mistakes. Hence,

they will feel rejected and unloved. What you need to do is give positivity and reassurance into their life through words and actions. Do so by:

- telling them how loved they are
- telling them how important they are to you
- appreciating the good they do
- praising them
- doing creative exercises and activities with them

Most importantly, break it down and explain that their mother leaving has nothing to do with them. You must repeat this to them because you do not want the wound of abandonment fester within them.

- **Refrain from talking negatively about the absent mother.** This may sound difficult since you will be dealing with your own baggage of emotions, and, believe me, they will not be positive feelings. But do be mindful of keeping those feelings to yourself and not sharing them or projecting them onto your child. You see, your child is also experiencing feelings of abandonment and anger, so if you share your experience with them, it will only make things worse for everyone. If in the future there is a possibility for the absent mother to return and mend bridges, you do not want to muddy the child's mind.

- **Talk about good and positive memories.** If there are good memories of the absent mother, then do not hesitate to share them with your child. It will not do any harm. You see, these good memories might be the only memory for the child, and they will be able to hold on to it as they grow up.
- **Highlight the support system in their life.** Your family is not the culturally "normal" family, so your child will pick on the difference and will feel the void. Hence, you need to tell your child that all families are different and that is okay. Moreover, you need to highlight that while, yes, they do have an absent mother, there are other people in their life who care for them, such as a grandparent, an aunt, or an uncle. Clarify that this support system is not a replacement for their absent mother but people who are present in their life and love them. This will make the child feel loved and wanted.
- **Equip your child with coping skills.** Not only is this important for a child with an absent

mother, but it is important for every child. When you teach your child coping mechanisms, they are better able to process and manage their negative emotions. You can do this by:

- telling them to be thankful for the things they have in life
- showing them different ways of thinking positively
- listing things that make them happy
- breathing techniques
- looking at tangible memories when upset

- **Seek professional help if needed.** Sometimes it will be beyond you to manage your child's emotions, and that is okay. Either the situation is beyond you, or your child is trying to protect you by not speaking to you. Whatever it may be, seek the guidance of a therapist. They are trained in their profession and know how to deal with such situations.
- **Look after yourself.** I know I say this quite often, but I cannot stress it enough. Take care of yourself as well. Dealing with so much can take a toll on you, so please make sure you are also happy while trying to make your children happy.

DEATH

Simply put, the death of a parent has a long-lasting impact on children. Usually, people do not know how to deal with death related grief in a child. You may wonder how to talk about the concept of loss and death and explain it to a child.

Effects

The impact on children of a parent's loss can lead to:

- **Inadequate Childcare:** After losing a parent, the child may face inadequate childcare as the surviving parent is suffering from the loss and may not being able to give their full attention.
- **Extra Responsibilities:** For older children, when they see their parents grieving and unable to function or process the loss, they tend to take on more responsibilities to manage things. This eventually leads to the child taking on more than what they should, which increases their stress and isolates them from their social life.
- **Changes in Behavior:** Children who have lost a parent will be at a higher risk of going through anxiety, depression, and stress and will have a lot of sleep disturbances. Moreover, they may

perform poorly in school and have low self-esteem issues.

Of course, death is not expected, and once a child is faced with, it leads to shock and trauma. There are long-term effects of death on a child, hence you should provide a space for them to grieve and normalize, rather than shun, the process of grieving.

Coping

When recognizing the symptoms of grief in your child, you need to understand that each child will experience any death or loss differently depending on their personality, what has happened, and their age. There is no blanket way to deal with a child's grief. Grieving is a part of life; you grieve because you love someone. Children will display grief differently compared to adults:

- Some might be in denial.
- Some will regress. (restart sucking their thumbs, wetting their bed, etc.)
- Some might be displaying externalizing behaviors. (aggression, irritability, or anger)
- Some may not want to leave your sight at all. (separation anxiety)

At this point, the world does not seem like a safe place to them. So, what can you do for your child?

- **Give them the permission to feel joy.** You see, they are already grieving which is a heavy process for them. When they do have snippets of fun while playing or enjoying themselves with friends, they might feel guilty. We do not want our child to think they can never laugh or smile after losing someone. Hence, verbally relay this message to them, "I know you are sad and are grieving, but it is also okay to feel joy. These feelings can exist together."
- **Normalize the process of grieving.** Most times people are uncomfortable with the process of grieving; it could be due to various reasons. But you need to provide the space and safety for them to be able to talk about their grief without shame. Tell them it is okay to be sad!
- **Let them cry.** Crying over loss is healthy. It is our body's response to the sadness and shock. Please do not tell your child to not cry. If they are crying, let them—they should let out their bottled emotions. The one thing you should not do is tell them to not cry and be strong. That is emotionally damaging!
- **Give them a memory box.** Help them make a

memory box filled with all the things they associate with their deceased parent. It could be a box of happiness and comfort for them. It could be a picture, a gift, a trinket, or anything they associate with the departed individual.

- **Ask them how they would like to remember them?** Ask your child how they would like to remember their parent? You can help them plant a tree in their memory, do a remembrance service for them each year, or even do the departed parent's favorite activity when they miss them. This helps channel the child's feelings and energy toward a constructive use.
- **Help them come to terms with verbalizing their feelings.** Help your child talk about what is on their mind. Encourage them to put their feelings in words or drawings. Rather than keeping their feelings within and repressing them, motivate them to speak about it and then receive those feelings openly. This is healthy in the long run as well.
- **Check in with them.** Check in with your child from time to time. Do not assume that they are okay or upset; ask them how they are feeling instead. Through this they will also be comforted knowing you are there to check up on them.

Grieving Their Mother on Mother's Day

When Darnell's children celebrated their first Mother's Day without their mother, it was heavy and painful. They were hesitant, but Darnell reminded them how their mother would have liked them to celebrate her. We were all there to support them, and we made it a habit to celebrate each year.

It will not be easy, but please try to help your children focus on the happy and positive memories of their mother. You see, your child has already lost their mother, but we do not want them to lose the emotional connection and memories of her. Helping to foster this bond will be beneficial for your child in the long run.

You can help your child partake in the following activities to grieve and celebrate their mother on Mother's Day:

- Make and adorn a memory box. Your child can fill it with belongings that remind them of their mother, such as jewelry, photographs, a book, a poem, or a clip.
- Help them write a letter. They can tell their mother what they have been doing since she passed away along with anything else they want to tell her. You could take them to the cemetery

and tell them to read it aloud to her, only if they are comfortable.
- Pretend to make a phone call to heaven to speak to their mother. This is a therapeutic way for your child to have a make-believe conversation with their mother and speak to her about whatever they like.
- Stick to following family traditions that their mother thought were important on Mother's Day, such as making a certain breakfast.
- Cook their mother's favorite dish and share it with everyone in the family.
- Make a memory book of their mother with photographs. They can pick which photographs to include.
- Write a story on their mother and add drawings.
- Play her favorite song and dance to it.
- Get a picture frame (you can even make one) and frame a picture of their mother in it.
- Contact their mother's relatives and friends and ask them to share their favorite and funniest memories with them.

Most importantly, give your child the space to talk and grieve for their mother. Provide them with active listening and remind them they will always have a mother who loved them. Do not leave this just for Mother's Day; keep it an ongoing communicative space for your child.

What do You Say When a Child Loses a Mother?

It is not easy to speak to your child after they have lost a parent. Moreover, you also have the difficult task of explaining what death is or where they are now. There will be questions. I spoke to a few fathers about how they spoke to their child and what they said to them when their mother passed away. I am sharing a few conversations below:

"I am hurting and in pain just as you are. Your mother left me behind along with you. I share your sadness, and I want you to know that you are not alone in this."

-Derek F. (Boston)

"Your mommy is in heaven now. She is watching over you like a guardian angel and will always love and protect you. I know you are upset, but remember, she is in our hearts."

-Lloyd B. (Phoenix)

"You will feel a lot of feelings, and they will not be easy to deal with, but please don't keep them inside. Talk to me about them; talk to anyone you think you can. I have a lot of feel-

ings about it as well, but we can be together as a family during this time."

-Richard P. (Detroit)

"I told my daughter that I had some bad news, and she thought I was joking. I wish I was, but I told her that your mom passed away. My voice barely came out and I started crying and so did she. It was not easy."

-Chris M. (Omaha)

It will not be easy my friend. You never recover from a loss. It stays with us, but we must learn to process it and grieve. You will need to be there for your child, and it will be challenging, but I know you can do it.

STRATEGIES TO REMEMBER FOR ANY TYPE OF LOSS

The journey of divorce or the loss of parent is a difficult and challenging transition for you and your child. I have covered how to help your child cope, but I want to take it a step further and give you tips on how to reinforce those coping mechanisms.

Following are some specific strategies through which you can help your child cope with either divorce or loss.

Drawing

Your child will be feeling a multitude of emotions and they may struggle to express them. What you can try is asking them to draw what they feel and then ask them to explain what they have drawn. Ask them to draw their feeling, their family, or their home. Ask them questions such as:

- What have you drawn?
- What does it mean?
- Please explain this to me.

Initiate a Conversation

Communication is important, especially honest communication. Keep the space for conversation open and accessible. Lead your child toward a good conversation during dinner, bedtime, or during a walk. If they are hesitant to bring up the topic, ask them:

- How do you feel about the divorce?
- How are you feeling?
- Has your life changed after the divorce?
- Let's talk about the positive.

- Let's talk about the negative.

Communicating From Afar

When the divorced parent moves away, it can become difficult for the child to see or communicate as much with the parent. You do not want your child to feel abandoned or cut communication with their mother. It is your job to help them:

- email
- video chat
- write letters
- send voice notes

Exercise

Partaking in activities together will help you spend time with your child. Moreover, if it is exercise, it can help your child, as well as you, channel angry feelings in a healthier manner. Exercising helps with the release of endorphins, so it leaves you feeling happier as well. Activities you and your child can do together are:

- swimming
- biking
- walking
- hiking

- camping
- skating

Playing Together

Playing with your child can create a space for them to speak to you since the environment is easier and less tense. You can:

- Engage in role play: Act out tough situations and see how to deal with them in a healthy manner.
- Play games: Your child will open up more easily during play time.
- Make puppets: Use puppets to voice feelings and do role play.

Read Together

There are numerous children's books on divorce. You can read them to your child or along with your child to help them process their feelings about your divorce. Because children can identify with book characters, they will be able to relate and verbalize how they are feeling.

Write Stories

Some children are creative with writing stories. If your child likes to write, then encourage them to write about their feelings. They can even draw pictures. If they are comfortable, then ask them to read the story out to you and discuss it with them.

Create a Personal History Timeline

It is natural, not only for children but adults as well, to worry about the future and what may happen now that the family structure is not the same. Worrying about things going back to "normal" is common. Help them make a chronological timeline; this will help them put their lives in perspective. They will be able to see the good experience in the past and anticipate future good experiences as well. Show them that life has good and bad experiences, but they will be able to process this with your support and love.

Make Two Secure and Loving Homes

You need to make your child comfortable in your home as well as your ex-partner's. You and your ex-partner can make sure that both homes have familiar belongings for your child, such as:

- favorite toys
- school supplies

- clothes
- favorite food
- pictures of the family

This creates a flow and familiarity for the child, which is comforting.

Have Parent Information Cards

Print out information cards for your family members. Through this, everyone will know how to contact the other. This will reassure your child. Write down your name, address, phone number, the number of days your child lives with each parent, and the activities they enjoy together.

Make a Time Capsule

Time capsules are a fun activity. They are also a constructive way to help your child understand and accept that divorce does not last forever, and life will have numerous things to look forward to. You can help your child collect the items they want to place in the time capsule such as a story, photograph, or treasures. You can also ask them some questions and put answers to those in the time capsule:

- Who are your friends?
- Name your family members

- What do you like doing?
- What do you want to do in the future?

Seal the time capsule, ask them when they want to open it, and then bury it.

Now you have a few strategies in your toolbox to help you and your child deal with missing a parent. In the next chapter I will go into detail on how to manage time and be better at organizing as a single father.

3

SINGLE-DAD GUIDE TO TIME MANAGEMENT AND ORGANIZATION

The stereotypical structure of a family is reliant on the father earning and the mother running the house and looking after the children. It is also common for both partners to work and divide tasks between each other. That is what Darnell and his wife did; hence, it was more difficult for him when all the responsibility fell on his shoulders after his wife passed away.

The burden can be overwhelming and exhausting, so I want to walk you through how you can manage your new responsibilities calmly and skillfully.

School transportation, preparing meal plans, getting the children's homework done, and traveling for sports —these were all the things Darnell had to juggle while continuing to work and take care of the household chores. When I would get time to see him, he was like a zombie running on reserve energy. He would only sleep around five hours a night, which was taking a toll on his health. His work was suffering, and he was more stressed, which he projected onto his children. No matter how much I helped or tried to offer, it was not enough because it was not a sustainable system. He needed to manage his time better, be more organized, and have a routine which did not adversely affect his health.

Mirabelle and I warned him. We told him that he was going to have a nervous breakdown or collapse if he didn't slow down. And eventually that is what happened. One day, he called me crying and breathing heavily and said, "I don't think I can do this Alfie. I want to give up, and I just can't go further." Those were not easy words to hear.

After that conversation, Darnell learned to be more mindful of his thresholds and his energy. He began to manage time more effectively, take time for himself, delegate tasks, ask for support, and organize more effectively. Of course, there were ups and downs, but the ups outnumbered the downs. And I want the same for you. You are the sole caregiver for your children now, so you need to be in the best mental and physical health.

MANAGING YOUR TIME

Parenting from the get-go is tough. It starts with sleep training, feeding, sleepless nights, bath time, potty training, school, and so on. It is an exhausting process until they become old enough to look after themselves. Imagine doing this alone, without the help of a partner.

The key to doing this—without losing your mind—is time management and organization. Why is time management so important? Time is your most precious resource. It is the core skill which so many things in your life depend on. Your first step is to set goals in the major areas of your life:

- family and personal goals
- business and career goals
- personal development goals

Once you have set these goals, decide how you want to divide your time amongst these categories. Where do you want to give the most time? To make this important decision, there are three questions to ask yourself:

- What is important to me?
- What are the things that give me the most pleasure and satisfaction?
- What is the most valuable use of my time right now?

You may need to revisit these questions as your circumstances continually change. This will help to keep your life in balance and time in check.

At Home

To help you, I have compiled a list of the top 10 household management tips for single fathers.

1. **Be proactive, not reactive.** What does this mean? You need to anticipate your child's needs and wants before things go downhill. Usually, children will be cranky if they have not slept well or eaten. You can avoid drama by avoiding both of those situations.
2. **Establish a routine for your child and yourself.** Design a routine that works well for your child and you. Include their school time, extra-curricular activities, homework, meals, and everyone's bedtimes. This way, you know exactly how the day will look like for everyone, and everyone is running on the same schedule.

You will do less running around with a system in place.

3. **Fill in the gaps.** If your child has soccer practice at 6:00 PM, schedule your grocery run, exercise, nap, or therapy session within that window of time. Overlapping activities can give you room to breathe while your child is engaged elsewhere.
4. **Ask for help.** When you have a support system in place, things are more manageable. Please do not shy away from asking for help; it makes life much easier. Alternate school pick up days with a school mother or father. Ask your parents or siblings to come once a month and babysit or chaperone your child while you take a day off.
5. **Make to-do lists.** A to-do list is a great way to save time and remember what you must do. It is natural to forget things over the course of a busy day; hence, a to-do list serves as a soft reminder and sets the tone for the day.
6. **Plan.** Write your goals (short-term and long-term) and work around those. If your child has a bake sale at school, write that down and be prepared well in advance. If you have a long day at work, plan to have your child picked up from school and ask a family member or friend to babysit until you get free. Prepare school meals

in advance and freeze foods. Even plan your outfits for the week—believe me when I say this saves time.

7. **Say no!** If you don't set boundaries and rules, it will be difficult to manage time. You must learn to say no and stick with it. I don't mean that you must be a harsh disciplinarian, but you cannot be too lenient.
8. **Delegate tasks.** If your child is old enough to help you, then ask them to pitch in. Tell them to have their room clean, set the table, wash the dishes, and so on. By asking them to help, you are also teaching them responsibility and ownership.
9. **Work with urgency, not panic.** Remember, do not panic! Half your energy will be diverted toward panicking, and this slows you down. Yes, you are working with an agenda, so you can be efficient but do not panic. You are capable and can manage.
10. **Wake up 20 minutes earlier than your child.** Yes, this sounds annoying, but it helps. If you give yourself some alone time before the house becomes active and noisy, it will set a good tone for the day. You can pull back your wake-up time according to your comfort and utilize that time for:

- self-care
- bath time
- meditation
- exercise
- making breakfast

When you are working on a time crunch, you will be overwhelmed. Remember, this does not make you a bad father. You are doing the best you can, and I need you to remind yourself of that! Give yourself a pat on the back for making it this far.

At Work

It is challenging to be managing your child, running a household, and working at the same time. I want to share how you can manage your job while juggling all the other responsibilities in your life.

Think about your most pressing pain point.

What does your job require of you? Do you have to travel a lot for your job? Is it possible to manage your boss's demands with your home life? Does your job have flexible hours? Figure out these dynamics so you can decide how to manage your time.

When you need help, ask for it.

If the nature of your work allows you to share the workload, don't hesitate to ask your colleague for help. In return, offer the same help when they need it. By the same token, if you must travel frequently for your job, have a trustworthy and functioning support system for when you are not in town.

Be an advocate for yourself.

If you have a boss that demands a lot of time, speak to them and fill them in on your situation. If your job does not have flexible hours, speak to the HR department, and ask how you can work around it. One of the most important and desired aspects about a job are flexible work hours and time off. You can ask them for earlier start and finish times or bargain longer but fewer days during the week—whatever suits your lifestyle. Remember:

- Center the request on how their work will benefit. Make sure you inform them how the request you are making is going to be of value to them. For instance, taking an extra day off will make you more focused and productive.
- Address your boss's concerns and fill them in on what your schedule will be and how you will work with the team.

- Propose a trial period for the changes you request. That will help your employer ease into the idea and see if it works for them.

Know that you have options.

If your current job is proving difficult to manage because of the time or workload, look for a new job. Do your research and see what suits you in terms of time—part-time, working from home, etc. Research companies, speak to existing employees, and find out what the work environment is like.

When searching, ask about the time flexibility. Is it rigid or open to change? Inquire about paid leave, sick leave, work-life balance, and child-care support. However, be wary of mentioning that you are a single father from the get-go since it might not work in your favor. You can also investigate freelance or part-time jobs. If you can utilize your skills to do freelance work, that would be beneficial for you. Moreover, you can also look for a part-time job which pays well and has shorter hours.

Basically, if your existing job is working out well for you in balancing home and work life, that's great! If not, please know that you can find another job. It may seem like a daunting task, but having a good and understanding work environment makes a big difference. By having an employer who allows flexibility and leniency, your home and work life will be much easier to manage. Nothing is impossible.

HOUSEHOLD ORGANIZATION

Now that we have covered how to manage your time and your job better, let's move on to how to manage your household more effectively!

Delegate Chores and Duties

As I mentioned earlier, delegate to your children if they are old enough. Map out weekly responsibilities and choose a day for cleaning together to keep it a fun activity. You can make a chart together and have a small reward system. These rewards do not have to be physical rewards, they could be watching a movie together, extended playtime, or a treat. Here are some of the tasks you can delegate to your children—depending on their ages.

- picking up and storing toys
- making the bed
- folding laundry
- dusting
- washing the dishes
- taking out the garbage

- vacuuming

Plan Meals

Rather than deciding what to eat an hour before lunch or dinner, make a weekly meal plan and stick it on the fridge. Shop for your groceries accordingly. If you are not the best at cooking, keep your meals simple to cook rather than taking on more challenging recipes. Two simple tips to keep in mind:

- Make a large amount and freeze it so that all you must do when you are too tired to cook is defrost, heat, and eat!
- If you go early in the morning around 8 AM or at night around 8 PM, you will be saved from long lines. Better yet, get your groceries delivered through delivery applications.

Make a Schedule

By making a schedule, you will be better prepared for the next day rather than doing any last-minute errand. Make your child pack their bag the evening before, ask them if they have anything planned, and be ready for the week ahead. Try these quick tips to help:

- **Get Automated:** No, I don't mean become a robot. I mean use technology to your advantage. If you have the finances, buy a dishwasher, rather than washing the dishes yourself. Invest in a robot vacuum cleaner and do any other errand or relax while it vacuums your house. If you have a garden, get a sprinkler and a robotic mower. It will free up time for you.
- **Carpool:** Coordinate pick-up and drop-off schedules with other parents. This not only works for school but extracurricular activities as well.

USE TECHNOLOGY TO YOUR ADVANTAGE

Utilize what you can to make life easier for yourself. Download time management applications and use them. I have compiled a list for you to save you time.

1. Cozi

This app has a shared calendar, and you can even set reminders for events. You can make to-do lists, shopping lists, meal plans, and it has a family journal where you can write memories.

2. Week Calendar

You can view your to-do lists and schedules by week, month, and year. Moreover, you can sync it with all your existing apps, such as iCloud and Google calendar. You can even share events with your contacts.

3. TeuxDeux

This app has a lovely check off and edit option, and most importantly, incomplete tasks are automatically carried on to the next day's tasks. Apart from a weekly task schedule, it even has a "someday bucket."

4. Toodledo

This app is slightly more structured. It enables you to make a hotlist of the most important tasks and enables filters to help you concentrate on specific tasks. Then, a scheduler helps figure out which task is more important based on your time and priority.

5. Big Oven

This is an app which allow you to save your favorite recipes, make grocery lists, and make meal plans for months in advance. One amazing feature about this app is that it even gives you meal ideas based on the leftovers you have in your kitchen.

REAL LIFE EXPERIENCES OF SINGLE FATHERS

I reached out to a few single fathers and asked them what advice they would like to give to other single fathers out there about time management and organization. This is what they had to say:

"Honestly, no matter how much you plan, which you should do, be prepared for anything and everything. But there will be days when things will not go according to plan—your child will fall sick, so you'll have to take a day off from work, or the fridge stopped working and your weekend chores are overlooked getting your fridge fixed. But remember, it is not the end of the world, you can do it!"

- John D. (Louisville)

"Look after yourself every day. You will come up with excuses like 'I don't have time' or 'my children are more important', which is understandable. But the entire point of time management and organization is so you can carve out time for yourself as well. There is no pride in working overtime and overdrive."

- Paul M. (Columbus)

"Take out time for your children. You may be thinking, 'what is this guy on about, my entire life is dedicated to them', but when I say take out time, I mean take out quality time that does not have to do with pick and drop and driving them from one activity to the other. Take out time to sit with them, talk to them, and go for a walk with them and so on. You get the gist."

- Ruben R. (Jacksonville)

"Life goes by fast, and when you have so much going on it is easy to lose sight of what you really want in life. You are busy doing one task and then go on to the other one. So slow down even though you are constantly on the clock. Slow down, breathe, take a moment, and remind yourself why you do what you do. It won't seem as daunting, thankless, or monotonous."

- Jared A. (Denver)

I cannot stress how important it is that you manage your time effectively, for your own sake as well as your family's. Without it, you will face a lot of challenges that could have been avoided. In the next chapter, I am going to dive into how to manage your finances as a single father.

4

SINGLE-DAD GUIDE TO MANAGING FAMILY FINANCES

Darnell is a banker, and his wife used to work part-time in a neighborhood bakery. While both had jobs, it was Darnell's income that they used to run the house and pay other expenses. His wife's money went toward their savings. When she passed away, and expenses increased, he started using up their savings.

He wasn't too happy with this, but he didn't have much of a choice. I prodded him to start thinking about budgeting, part-time gigs, and insurance. He was hesitant to begin with, but he slowly warmed up to the idea. Now, Darnell manages his finances like a professional.

I don't want to scare you, but according to the US Department of Agriculture, the cost for a middle-income couple to raise their child until their 18th birthday is around $241, 080. Financial stress is not easy, it affects the mental and physical well-being. "The link between financial hardship, poor health and poor mental health has been demonstrated in multiple populations" (Stack & Meredith, 2018).

Darnell is now efficient with budgeting, saving, and planning. It wasn't an easy journey for him, but deciding to take the first step is a step in the right direction.

FINANCIAL DIFFICULTIES AS A SINGLE FATHER

Many two-parent families struggle with managing finances, so how difficult does it get for a single parent? Financial struggles are nothing to be ashamed of; they are a part of life. When the paychecks go from two to one, it will be difficult. If you were able to go grab a coffee every day or eat lunch out every day, now you may not be able to because you must cut back on expenses. Some common struggles single fathers face are:

- **Paying Bills:** If you are not mindful of how you spend, the cost of bills will go up.
- **Savings:** You might be burning through

existing savings as a single father to make ends meet. I understand. With all the grocery, utility, childcare bills, it is not easy.

- **Childcare:** If you have a job and enroll your child in a daycare center, the cost of your expenses will go up.
- **Outings:** Weekend activities such as eating out, watching a movie, and so on can be expensive.
- **Debt:** You might rack up debts if you find yourself taking loans.
- **Budgeting:** You don't have time to sit down and budget, so everything is going haywire.

HOW TO MANAGE FINANCIAL DIFFICULTIES

Now that we know what sort of financial difficulties a single father can be faced with, we will investigate how to deal and overcome them.

Paying Bills

You can bring the cost of bills down. Call the requisite supplier and ask them for a cost cut. However, to do this, you must have no contract. You can even switch to a supplier with better rates. And in terms of utilities, remember to keep the lights switched off and unplug electronics when you are not using them.

Savings

When you create a budget, you save. Figuring out rent, utilities, and food will help you understand how much money is being spent. Whatever you have left, even if it is a small amount, put it toward savings. (*I want to give you a tip: you can have a look at cashback websites and save money when you need to buy things.) Even if you only put $50 per month toward savings, do it! No amount is too small. You could have it automatically cut from your monthly salary or have it automatically transferred to your savings account. Having more than one savings account also helps, such as ones labeled childcare, emergency, and recreational.

Childcare

Childcare is expensive. According to Child Care Aware of America, nearly 36% of a single parent's salary goes towards childcare. However, it differs depending on your location and number of children. The usual cost of childcare ranges from $9,100 to $9,600 annually for one child.

Luckily, there are ways of obtaining a certain percentage of free childcare or requesting tax-free childcare. Find out if you are qualified for The Child Care and Development Fund assistance. The government also provides tax provisions such as exemptions and deductions through childcare tax exclusions and the dependent care assistance program. Furthermore, you can also check out in-home care which may be less expensive. However, always make sure the organization is certified.

Outings

Let's face it, family outings as a single parent are financially heavy. Watching a movie, going to the skating rink, going to the mall, and so on will be tough on your wallet. Look for deals, discount coupons, and discount websites. It may be more effort, but it will be worth it. Plan trips that do not require much spending, such as a picnic in the park, a day at the beach, a hike through nature, a skate at the park, or a ride on a bike.

Debt

You might be running late on payments or borrowing money; hence, what you owe is more than what you earn. Look into a voluntary payment plan, a debt relief order, a debt management plan, or look into the Temporary Aid for Needy Families program (TANF). Once you have made a budget, see where you can save money and put it aside to pay debt off.

Budgeting

This is one of the most important aspects of managing finances. If you can figure out exactly how much you spend and where you spend it, you will be well equipped to figure out the remaining issues.

- **Set a Financial Goal:** This could be working toward a better car, saving for a house, or going on a holiday. It will help keep you accountable for your actions and help you remain more focused.
- **Know Your Money:** Know exactly what is coming in every single month and what is going out every month. What is your financial month (the day you get paid)? This date marks the starting point of when expenses begin.
- **Pay bills on Time**: Know that you must put a certain amount of money aside for bills (rent, electric, water, and debt) and then work backward. You need to have the roof over your head and your electricity and gas going before anything else. You can cut that amount from your salary and pay the bills in the first week after getting paid.
- **Buy Food Last:** Keep the money aside for food, but only go grocery shopping once you have paid your bills.

- **Create a Gift Account:** Budget for birthdays and Christmas. Know how much you will spend on these occasions. It is so easy to get caught up in excitement during these times. Think about what you are spending, know your limit, and stick to it. Discuss it with your child if they are old enough.
- **Avoid Phone Contracts:** Get a sim card which needs a monthly top up. It means you have better control over your finances.
- **Clear Your Debt:** When debts are cleared, financial worries are lessened since you don't have to pay interest. This is great for your financial and mental health.
- **Open a Savings Account:** Commit to saving a certain amount each month, no matter what.
- **Meal Plan:** It makes a difference to the cost of food you purchase. When you know exactly what you are eating, you will buy only those ingredients rather than wasting on others.

It will take time, planning, effort, and patience, but you will be able to do it. Once you get into the habit of making a budget and sticking to it, believe me, you will be much happier.

HOW TO EARN EXTRA MONEY AS A SINGLE FATHER

If your job offers flexibility and if you have the time and energy to make some extra money on the side, then I would suggest you do it. You don't have to go out to do any work; rather, you can do it within the comfort of your home. However, you will need time, organization, and focus to do this. I have compiled a list of side jobs you can do to make extra money:

1. **Affiliate Marketing:** All you do is promote other companies or brand's products and get a cut from any sales. Some websites that offer this are: Rakuten, Linkshare, Amazon, Clickbank, and JVZoo.
2. **Listen to Music:** Listen to any unsigned band, write a review on them, and submit it at Slicethepie.
3. **Freelance Writing:** Check out Upwork or Elance to get writing gigs.
4. **Garage Sale:** If you have any extra items or clutter in the house, have a garage sale.
5. **Resell Books:** Check out BooksCouter.com and assign them to sell all your old books and magazines.

6. **Trying new Products**: Companies and brands will pay you to review and use their product.
7. **Fiverr:** You can design a logo, write a resume, write a short story and make money.
8. **Mystery Shopper:** You will earn money to shop at brands and stores by acting as a shopper and surveying the market.
9. **Type and Earn:** SpeakWrite allows you to take shifts where you have to transcribe.
10. **Teach Online:** If you think you are good at graphic designing or marketing, sign up with Udemy or Skillshare and teach to earn money.

See what works best for you in terms of time and effort. There will be some trial and error, and you won't start making a lot of money right away, so be patient with the process.

TIPS FOR COPING WITH FINANCIAL STRESS

Suffering from financial stress has a negative impact on your health, mind, and family. It leads to foregoing health care, mental health issues, medical issues, and negative coping behaviors. What are some healthy ways to cope?

- Earn extra money through side jobs. (I have provided a list.)
- Seek therapy.
- Break your debt cycle through awareness.
- Keep a check on your budget.
- Ask for mental support from family and friends.
- Join a support group for people dealing with financial stress.
- Take out time to unwind by doing whatever relaxes you.

APPLYING YOUR SKILLS

"Knowledge is useless without consistent application"

— JULIAN HALL

Now that you have read up on how to save and earn money, it is time for you to apply it and benefit from your new knowledge. Download a budgeting app such as Mint, Goodbudget, or YNAB. I have also included a budget sheet to help you with your finances. Get going!

My Budget Worksheet

Monthly Budget for: _____

Income	Details (earned from etc)	Amount	My Notes
Paycheck Income			
Other Income			
	Total Income		

Category	Details Account names etc.	Budgeted Amount	Actual Spent	Difference Amount under / over	My Notes
Long Term / Emergency Savings					
Retirement					
Emergency Fund					
Essentials / Needs					
Mortgage / Rent					
Home Insurance					
Auto Insurance					
Electricity					
Water					
Gas					
Phone					
Groceries					
Other:					
Other:					
Other:					

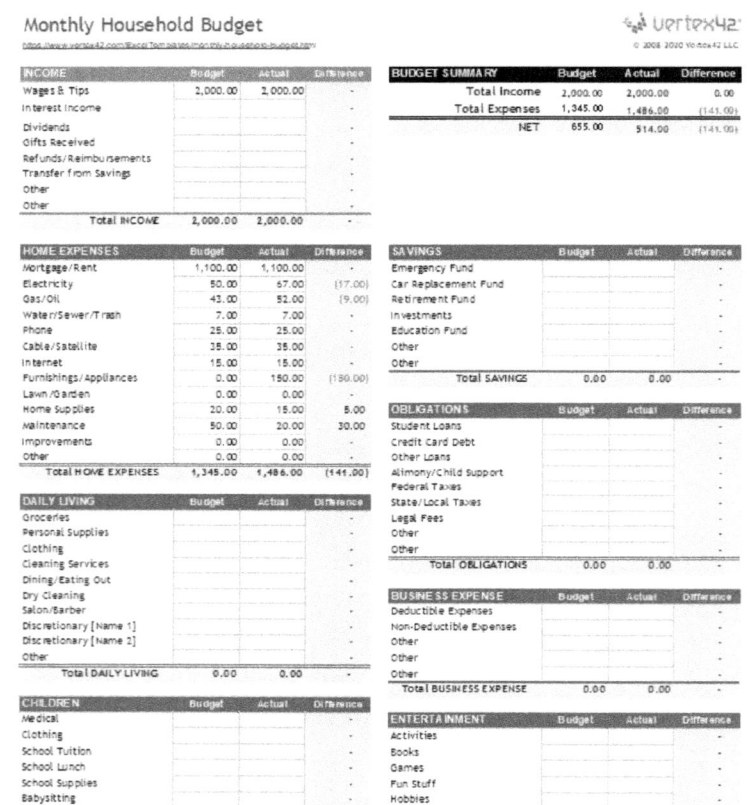

REAL LIFE EXPERIENCES OF SINGLE FATHERS

I interviewed and spoke to single fathers about their financial worries, following is the advice and help they offered:

"One of the most important things is to make use of government assistance. It could be food, aid, or job related, but I *believe it really helps. That extra help is a miracle. It will take a bit of time to receive it, but it is worth the wait."*

- Roger F. (Philadelphia)

"Childcare will be difficult, I have two children, and when my wife passed away, it was difficult to raise them while managing a job and the house. But I reached out to my family to babysit and also utilized the Childcare Assistance Program which covers the cost of childcare. It became more manageable in terms of money and time with the programs help."

- Joshua P. (Ohio)

"Where do I start? Budgeting was a nightmare. Household chores were weighing me down, and childcare had me stressed out. But I began to prioritize. I forced myself to make a budget because everyone I spoke to said it was the most important aspect to managing my finances. So, I made one! And boy did it change my situation. I was also calmer and less edgy. Please make a budget!"

- Steven G. (Kentucky)

"Don't stress. Yeah, that would be my most important advice. Financial stress is a killer, and it is so easy to get caught up

in it, become depressed, and project it onto your children and whatnot. So, just remind yourself that you can manage it and handle it. Rather than worrying, do something, take concrete steps towards changing your situation."

— Scott E. (Toledo)

By now, you know that financial struggles are a given as a single father. But you also know there are ways out of it. I have provided you with numerous tips and strategies to improve your financial situation, so rest assured, you will see results once you begin taking steps. In the next chapter I will cover how to be the best single father to your daughter.

5

BEING A SINGLE DAD TO A DAUGHTER

Dominique, Darnell's daughter, was 13 years old when she lost her mother. She was at an already challenging time for her in terms of body, emotional, and hormonal changes. She missed her mother a lot, and it was evident. She was an energetic and creative child, but she became quiet and withdrawn after her mother's demise. She stopped meeting her friends, stopped going to her extracurricular activities, and remained in her room for hours. It was difficult for Darnell to witness that change in Dominique.

While Mirabelle did offer her support and time to Dominique, it wasn't the same as a mother's love and support. At first, Darnell let it slide and avoided it because he had a lot on his plate. He was also scared because he felt he would not be able to handle his daughter's sadness. But he realized this was not the healthiest way to approach the situation. His therapist told him to face the situation rather than avoid it because if Dominique didn't get help now, it would cause long-term mental health issues.

Darnell began to take small steps towards addressing his daughter's situation. To begin with, he took out time to communicate with her, asked her to verbalize what she was feeling, spent quality time with her, and enrolled her in grief counseling sessions. At first Dominique was hesitant and resistant, but we noticed a visible change in her. She began to regain the vivacity she had lost, and while we knew she missed her mother and harbored the pain of loss, she spoke about it rather than repressing it.

THE HARDEST PART

There is no perfect or proven way to raise children. You do the best you can with whatever resources you have. It is easier with a partner, but when you are left alone to do the job, it can be overwhelming, and you may be lost and confused.

Not that we need to differentiate based on gender, but sometimes it creeps in. It is a reality. It is naturally assumed that mothers are closer to their daughters because of the female bond and connection, but that isn't entirely true. Fathers can create a bond with their daughters as well. There are numerous challenges single fathers face while raising a daughter:

- **Gender Stereotypes:** You will be viewed through an unfair gender lens. Most people think you are already doing a good enough job by just being present and taking on the responsibility. Men are viewed from a pitied and harsher lens, "Will he be able talk to her about girly issues?" "Will he be able to connect emotionally with his daughter?" Comments from others like: "Oh, she must miss her mother. It isn't the same with fathers" don't help. There will be constant judgment and comments from others.
- **Difficult Discussions:** Talking about puberty, menstruation, dating and sex brings a certain awkwardness. Your daughter may be uncomfortable speaking about it with you.
- **Being Present:** Not having enough communication or being part of her daily life can be a struggle. With difficulty in communication, it can be easy to ignore the things your daughter does in her daily life.
- **Lack of Confidence:** You will find yourself

questioning your abilities. Death doesn't come announced; hence, when you lose a partner, you are thrown into the single parenting mode right away. There is a lot to learn.

- **Loneliness:** You may think you are the only one facing these challenges while everyone is acing it. But remember, we all are learning and growing every day. You are not alone!
- **Overprotectiveness:** It is easy to get carried away with being overprotective with your little girl. This can put a strain on your relationship.

OVERCOME THE CHALLENGES OF RAISING YOUR DAUGHTER

While there are challenges, there are also ways to work around them, so do not worry, I have it covered for you.

Gender Stereotypes

How others view you should not be of any concern to you. You need to support yourself and your decisions and be confident in them. There will be numerous people who pass judgements, but remember, you are the one living the situation, not them. Make it a point not to personalize other people's judgements. Hearing thoughtless comments hurts, because here you are, trying your best and giving it your all, and someone comes along and bursts your balloon. We cannot control what others will say, but we can control our reaction and learn to block their negative opinions. Remind yourself you are doing the best you can and give yourself constant validation.

Difficult Discussions

De-stigmatize the conversations around puberty and menstruation and keep communication open and honest. Your reaction to these topics will affect the communication, so be mindful. Do your research. Speak to other women about their experiences and how they would approach the topic. Go with your daughter to buy pads and tampons. Give them support when they are menstruating be open to what they have to say or questions they may have.

As for menstruation specifically, be aware of their physical and hormonal changes. Do not shy away from knowing they will develop breasts, they will develop feminine curves, they will observe hair growth, and they will experience mood swings. Yet again, do your research, speak to other women, and make space for the conversation. If you think it is going to be awkward, it will be; so, I suggest you treat it as a normal conversation rather than psyching yourself up about it. Moreover, ask them to read and research on it as well and sit and have a dialogue about what they learned and what you know. During these changes, please ask how she is feeling, rather than assuming.

Make sure you convey your rules about dating and sex through assertive talk. It is not a negative topic, so don't address it with that mind-set. Normalize the topics, so your daughter feels comfortable turning to you when needed. Speak to her about safe sex, respecting her body, respecting her boundaries, communicating her boundaries, and being in control of her decision.

Being Present

Unfortunately, men are conditioned to not express feelings. Therefore, communication can become difficult. So, there's a lot of unlearning to do. Remember, to keep the space for communication open and honest. Make it known that she can speak to you. Sometimes, rather than a solution, your daughter will just want you to act as her sounding board. Ask her what her need is, show empathy, and provide her with active listening and patience. This will build a strong bond between you two.

Sometimes we get caught up in our lives, sometimes your child doesn't want to share, and sometimes we just don't know what is going on in our child's life. But be involved in your daughter's life as much as possible.

Show her that you are interested and support her hobbies and interests. Take out time to go shopping with her, go for a walk together, cook your favorite meals together, attend her school events, and ask her about her day and her friends. This allows you to know more about your daughter and will strengthen the bond between you two.

Lack of Confidence

We've all been there—in every facet of life. We think we do not know enough and worry we are not doing a good enough job. However, the new situation you find yourself in is going to be a lesson on its own. You will learn on this journey, you will make mistakes, but you will do the right thing. So, remember to be patient with yourself. Nobody lands up in such situations knowing everything. They do not come with a manual.

Loneliness

You are never alone! Accept and acknowledge that this is not the easiest job and when it does get overwhelming for you, you can ask for support and help. It doesn't make you less of a man or a bad father, it just makes you human. Reach out to friends, family, or a support group.

Overprotectiveness

This is an instinct, but you must learn to keep it under control and be mindful of when it is needed and when it is not. Challenges and problems are a part of life, and as tough as it sounds, there will be times when you will need to let your child take the challenge and learn from it rather than rescue them. Overprotectiveness can lead to your daughter becoming very dependent on you or becoming rebellious. Give her space, have faith in her ability to stand up to challenges, have faith in her ability to self-soothe, and allow her to come to you to ask for help rather than jumping in straight away. This will encourage self-confidence. She will learn to believe in herself while knowing you are there if she needs your help.

DOING YOUR BEST

Now that you know the challenges and how to overcome them, it is time to put your single father skills and knowledge into practice. Remember my friend, Rome wasn't built in a day. Have patience with yourself and begin to cultivate positive parenting habits. The following is a list of things you can do and say to raise your daughter in a healthy manner:

1. Praise her looks, but don't stop there. She needs to know that appearance is not the only important aspect in her life. Compliment her creativity, intelligence, humor, and strength.
2. Teach her how to be resourceful and how to handle jobs that are meant to be "men's jobs." First things first, there is no such thing as men's jobs and women's jobs. Teach her how to change a bulb, write a check, perform routine car maintenance, and so on. Teach her how to be self-reliant.
3. Speak about women in a respectful manner. Remember, the way you portray women will have an important impact on your daughter's identity.
4. Be open about body parts and identify them correctly once she grows up.
5. Teach her honesty by being honest yourself.
6. Read her books with strong female heroes.
7. Teach her how to respect her own body. Tell her and remind her that her body is hers, and nobody can tell her what to do with it. Tell her to draw boundaries and support them unwaveringly.
8. Normalize topics such as dating, sex, and menstruation by talking about them without shame and awkwardness.

9. Swap your favorite hobbies once a week and see how you two like each other's hobbies.
10. Be silly and laugh over small mistakes. This will teach her to not be scared and fearful over mistakes.
11. Help her choose a female mentor whom she can trust and turn to if she feels she needs more support.
12. Help her find an inspirational woman she looks up to.
13. Have a good heart to heart conversation at least once a day.
14. Be open about the usage of alcohol and drugs. It is a part of life; she will try it at some point. Tell her the truth—anything done in moderation is okay. Draw healthy boundaries. If you overstep your boundary, it will negatively impact her physical, social, and mental health.
15. No means no! Teach her and show her what physical and emotional boundaries are.
16. Reassure and validate her with phrases such as "you have got this," and "you are doing great."
17. Give her space and privacy.
18. Give her the respect and attention she deserves by looking her in the eye while speaking to her and not being distracted by your mobile phone or the TV.

19. Do something together that is solely your time with her such as: going to the beach for a picnic every Sunday, going for ice-cream after Saturday breakfast, or going for a movie together.
20. Tell her you love her and show physical affection.

REAL LIFE EXPERIENCES OF SINGLE FATHERS

I interviewed and spoke to single fathers about how to raise a daughter single handedly. They offered the following advice:

"Just shed the awkwardness please! You will be doing yourself and her the biggest favor. We [Eric and his daughter] had already spoken about menstruation and puberty beforehand, so she came running to me as soon as she got her first period, and I went and bought her pads. It is normal if you treat it normally."

- Eric J. (Richmond)

"I reached out to my female friends and my sisters and mother. Whenever I would feel lost or cut off, I would ask them to advise me on how to take things forward. My daughter began dating and it was an odd place for me to be

at, so I asked my sister to give me tips on how to have a conversation with my daughter. All I wanted to say was be safe, don't get hurt and respect your body, which I conveyed keeping my sister's perspective in mind. Truth be told, there is no right way to have this conversation, just make sure you are understanding, open and honest."

- Dennis B. (San Jose)

"Oh boy was I protective about my daughter. I did not let her lift a finger when my ex-wife and I separated. I molly coddled her too much, until my mother pointed out that I need to let her be independent and start trusting her to make her own choices. When I did that, I noticed a whole new person, so allow your daughter to be who she is, let her personality develop without smothering it."

- Harold L. (Portland)

"There was a time when my daughter stopped speaking to me, didn't involve me in her life and shut me out. It hurt, I thought I was being a good father, but clearly, I wasn't. I let this slide thinking it was because she's a teenager and must be changing hormones, but it became worse. So, one day I sat her down and told her to speak to me, but it didn't work. So, I began to make small changes, such as dinner time conversation, going to her cheerleading practices, dropping her to the

mall, and so on—slowly she started allowing me into her life and opening up to me. It was all about showing attention and making small efforts to be a part of her life."

- Marcus C. (Fresno)

Raising your daughter alone, you will miss a female presence or wish your wife was around. But alas, it is just you. You do not need to fill the gap of a mother, but you can be the best possible father to your daughter by applying all that you have read. Remind yourself that you can do anything. In the next chapter, I will go in depth on how to be a great single father to your son.

6

BEING A SINGLE DAD TO A SON

Darius, Darnell's son, was only 11 years old when his mother passed away. He did not express his grief. Instead, he was always playing video games, watching shows, and chatting on his mobile phone. He shut himself off, just as Dominique did.

His grades at school were being affected, and at home he would be irritable and angry. On top of his own grief, Darnell had to manage his two children who were also experiencing grief. It was not easy. One day, Darnell received a call from the school; Darius had been in a fight with another boy. I suppose this was a wakeup call for Darnell, who then sat his son down and spoke to him. He enlisted him with a grief counselor for children and took out time every day to speak to him. Daily, he would ask him how he was feeling and how his day was. While initially Darius was averse to these changes, he began to warm up to them.

One night, over dinner, he burst out crying—something he had not done since his mother had passed away. Darnell saw this as a good sign. He was glad that Darius had finally let his emotions and grief come out in a healthy way instead of bottling up his anger. I think the most important thing Darnell did was normalize grief and take the time to talk to his children. Of course, Darius did not stop loving or grieving, but he knew he had a safe space with his father and counselor where he could verbalize his feelings.

Your influence on your child starts the day they are born, and as children grow up, you will hear them say, "I want to be just like daddy," or "I want to be just like mommy," so you know how important of a role model you are in their life. Now that you are parenting alone, you will need to be twice the role model.

YOUR IMPORTANCE AS A SINGLE FATHER

Sons learn a lot from their fathers, they identify their masculinity with their father and want to be like him when they grow up. Parenting styles between mothers and fathers are often different due to stereotypical gender responsibilities. The role of fathers has evolved over time to involve more than just being a breadwinner. Now, men are more involved with caregiving in a family. To fully embrace your paternal role, you must be active in many facets.

Being a sole caregiver and provider for your children can be a lot to take in and deal with. You will face numerous challenges. Be aware of how your fathering role has changed. Ask yourself how you were as a father before you lost your wife or got divorced? What was your role in your child's life? Were you an active participant in caregiving responsibilities, or were you only available for a goodnight kiss and weekend activities?

Neither mothers nor fathers are given a manual with the birth of their children. We do what we have been conditioned and taught to do. A father can read a baby's emotional cues just as well as a mother. Moreover, according to research, fathers play an active part of their son's emotional, cognitive, and physical development. You need to know that the more love, warmth, and openness you show towards your son, the fewer the problems your son will face in academics, relationships, drug related issues, and self-esteem issues. Your positive involvement in your son's life will benefit him for a lifetime.

You act as a role model for your child in terms of protection and economic safety and comfort. While your parenting style may not be the same as your deceased partner's or your ex-partners, know that the difference is important. According to research, father's love their children in a more dangerous manner. This is not in a scary dangerous manner. It simply refers to the fact that they play rougher games with their children rather than gentler ones. These rough and tough games naturally instill competition, independence, and risk-taking in the child. Moreover, your active participation in your son's life will provide a wider range of social experiences and help them deal with challenges in life with a more diverse skill set.

You will end up teaching your son about objectivity and the outcomes of right and wrong. You can provide them insight into the real world, prepare them for life, and teach them respect toward women.

Your son being male, does not mean they do not need love, affection, warmth, physical affection, and reassurance—they do. Hug them, tell them you love them, and make them feel safe and secure. If you are the type of person who does not show much affection, please sit and think about what made you that way. Try to take small steps towards changing it for your children.

RAISING A SON

How exactly can you influence your son to be a kind, well-adjusted, and good human? Well to begin with, you can't teach him everything, you can show him. As Steve Biddulph says, "To be a good man, you first need to see a good man." Steve Biddulph is a renowned psychologist and believes that around the age of six, fathers begin to make the most difference in their son's lives. According to him, there are three stages in a boy's upbringing:

1. **The Mother Stage (0 to 6 years):** At this point, mothers are the focal point of a boy's life.
2. **The Father Stage (6 to 14 years):** At this stage, boys begin to understand they are male and begin to look for role models. They observe and imitate their father's behavior. This stage is vital for fathers to make a positive difference in their son's life.
3. **The Mentor Stage (14 to 18 years):** Boys begin to transition into manhood because of an increase in testosterone levels. Fathers will feel a distance from their son's end since sons will now look to other mentors that are not their parents.

What You Do

Sometimes being the example is the best way to teach your son how to behave. Be the kind of man and do the kinds of things that you want him to do.

Take the Time

Please make it a point to take time and have heartfelt conversations with your son. Research indicates that fathers who do not give attention to their sons are making a grave error because lack of attention leads to misbehavior and more negative attention seeking behaviors. Simply take out some time during the day where you two can play, talk, go for a walk, and have a wholesome conversation. Your focus will have a positive impact and make your son feel special and loved, they will see that even though you are busy and working, you still have time for them.

Rough and Tumble Time

Wrestling and tough times are important! Boys love to play such games with their fathers. This play time helps them learn lessons such as strength, physical development, problem solving, and spatial awareness. If the wrestling gets out of hand, remember to stop and remind him to be careful because you don't want either of you to be hurt. This is an important lesson for them: when things are getting out of hand, slow down and ask where you need to channel your energy.

Be in Tune With Their Softer Side

While it is important to have rough and tough play time to show them their strength and problem-solving skills, it is equally important to help them regulate their feelings and emotions. Do not shun emotions with phrases such as: "boys don't cry," "boys are strong," or "boys will be boys."

Teach your son to honor his emotions, whatever they may be, rather than repressing them. If he is angry, ask him about why he is angry. If he is sad, ask him what he is upset about. Let them feel because when they become comfortable with their feelings, they will better be able to verbalize them and grow to become emotionally intelligent men. This goes for you to, don't just give lip service to these lessons, act them out. Your children will learn from your actions as much as any lecture.

Respect Women

The way you treat women will be emulated by your son —remember that. Lead by example and be mindful that your son is learning from you. It starts at home. How you speak about your ex-partner, how you refer to women, and how you behave toward women in general matters. You must teach them never to be aggressive or violent toward women and be mindful of their feelings and emotions.

What You Say

Moreover, what you say to your child also makes an impact on their lives.

1. Accept your mistakes and tell them, "I have failed as well, and it is okay."
2. "Your happiness comes before others, and it is not selfish; it is self-love."
3. "Please tell me honestly if this is your best effort?" This will make them understand that you know when they are not putting in their best and will encourage them to do better.
4. "Treat people the way you want to be treated." This will instill empathy and acceptance in them.
5. "Some things are beyond your control. Don't assume everything is your fault."
6. "I love you and understand where you are coming from."

This may seem a lot to take in, and it will take time for you to learn and then practice this. Be patient and take it one step at a time.

What You Teach

What exactly is right to teach your son? It is a subjective answer at the end of the day, so decide what is right for you and your son. Regardless, you will have to be consistent with your parenting method. Things that are universally important for you to teach your son include the following:

1. **Motivate him to dream.** Do not squash his dreams and let him dream big.
2. **Stand up after a fall.** I mean this metaphorically. Teach your son to accept failure, learn from it, and try again. Remind him it is okay to fail and praise him for his effort.
3. **Be a good sport.** Teach your son that he cannot always win at life. There will be challenges; hence, he must know how to lose gracefully.
4. **Teach appropriate displays of affection.** Affection is not just hugging and cuddling, it is also verbal affection. Show him his worth with praise, reassurance, validation, and physical affection as well.
5. **Stress the importance of a good work ethic.** Teach him responsibility by delegating chores.
6. **Instill good communication skills.** With the advent of mobile phones, good quality communication suffers. Teach your son how to

communicate effectively and in a healthy manner.

7. **Teach him good manners.** This is not a one-time parenting activity, this is lifelong. Lead by example, always say please and thank you, be okay with apologizing, and so on. These manners go a long way.
8. **Teach the importance of kindness.** Not only is kindness toward others important, but kindness to himself is as well. Tell him how bullying is wrong, helping others is right, and model kindness and gratitude yourself.
9. **Highlight the importance of not giving into peer pressure.** There will be times when your son will feel peer pressure, so you need to highlight the importance of drawing a boundary and making a decision. Teach him to say no and support his decision.
10. **Instill honesty.** Tell him the difference between a white lie and big lies, inspire being truthful, and stick to your word.
11. **Help him find his passion and talent.** Encourage his passions rather than discourage them and help him develop his talent.
12. **Teach him the importance of cleanliness.** This will also help him learn good grooming

habits. You need to tell him how to look after his body and environment.

13. **Teach him self-love and how to draw boundaries.** Self-love is relational to drawing boundaries. However, you must teach him to respect other people's boundaries as well.
14. **Don't focus on gender stereotypes.** Do not put your son in a box of masculinity. Let him explore his gender and set his own limits.
15. **Be actively involved in his school and academics.** Have regular meetings with his teacher, attend matches, monitor his homework, and ask about his day at school.
16. **Encourage his hobbies even if they are not typical for a boy.** If he is interested in ballet or fashion designing, please do not shut it down. Instead, motivate and encourage him to follow his passion. Remember, gender stereotypes are society's stifling norms, they do nothing but trap us in a box of conformity.
17. **Teach him the importance of making good life decisions.** Talk to your child about his goals and the choices he wishes to make in his life. Understand where he is coming from. Most importantly, set an example for him by making healthy choices yourself.

HEALTHY AND POSITIVE ACTIVITIES FOR YOU AND YOUR SON

As I have mentioned earlier, it is important to take out time to spend with your son. It might be difficult as a single father, since you already have so much going on, but it is possible. The following activities are a great way to spend quality time and engage with your son.

1. Read books with him and discuss them.
2. Play an instrument together.
3. Go camping.
4. Change a tire.
5. Have a BBQ in the backyard.
6. Teach him how to tie a tie.
7. Play a sport together.
8. Help him manage money.
9. Volunteer.
10. Go cycling.

These activities are a great way to spend time together, get in physical activity, and learn how to better communicate with your son.

REAL LIFE EXPERIENCES OF SINGLE FATHERS

I interviewed and spoke to single fathers about how to raise a son single handedly. This was their advice:

"To be honest, I was petrified. I was left to take care of my 5-year-old son when my wife left me. My life was all about work, so having to look after my son forced me to slow down and see what he needs (physically and emotionally). I thought I wouldn't be able to manage, would lose my job, would mess my son up, but it turned out fine, so while it may seem like a lot, which it is, remember you can do it."

- Walter A. (Pittsburgh)

"I had a hard time expressing my emotions towards my 15-year-old son. I knew he was in a tough place because his mother had passed away, but I felt awkward sitting and speaking to my son about how he felt. For some reason I thought it wasn't a 'manly' thing to do. But going to grief counseling really helped me debunk this stereotype and I began noticing a change in my son when I started opening up to him as well."

- Miguel J. (Reno)

"I hated it when everyone around me would say I can't be a good father to my son because that's not how I am built. I mean come on, who is anyone to pass that judgment? Initially, these judgments would hurt, and I ended up believing in them, but I realized what others say about me doesn't make me that way. And then onwards, I stopped personalizing it and started focusing on what I can do within my own limits to make my son happy."

- Paul A. (Buffalo)

"My father did not have a good relationship with me, and I swore to myself that I would not be the same with my son. So, I gave him my best and made sure not to repeat the same mistakes."

- Brendon L. (Irving)

Just like the bond between a mother and daughter is special, a father's relationship with his son is irreplaceable. How you raise your son will be momentous in his life. In the next chapter, I will go in-depth on how to raise a child with special needs as a single father.

7

BEING A SOLO PARENT TO A CHILD WITH SPECIAL NEEDS

You can choose to skip this chapter if you're not a parent to a child with special needs. Or better yet, immerse yourself in the knowledge contained within, and use it to help other single dads who may be in this situation. Being a single parent is not easy, and if you are a single parent to a child with special needs, it will be even more challenging.

A single father I interviewed for this book—Roger—has an autistic son. He said he struggled initially. He described his child as being extremely sensitive to the outside world. Everyday things such as noises, lights, and sounds would be problematic for his son. Moreover, his son would get anxious and stressed in unfamiliar surroundings, and he had difficulty expressing himself verbally. Autistic children need a very rigid routine; it can't be flexible. This was something Roger's wife used to handle. However, after she passed away, he was left alone to manage everything. He felt isolated, lost, and lacking for support.

However, Roger learned to adapt. He accepted the change and transitioned to adjust. He took on a work from home job with flexible hours and reached out for support in his family and community. He said nothing happened overnight—it was a process. Just believe you can do it and be patient with yourself.

THE CHALLENGES

There will be a lot of uphill struggles, some of which can only be understood by a parent in your unique situation.

1. **Your child requires more attention, dedication, and patience.** When your child is diagnosed, they will require extra time and energy which will be exhausting for you.
2. **There are no vacation days.** You can't take a day off to rest because you are always on your feet.
3. **People will offer unsolicited advice.** There will be people who will give off handed

comments such as, "take out time for yourself," or "practice more self-care."
4. **Finding adequate childcare is tough.** It will be difficult to find someone you can trust, someone who is well-informed about your child, and someone who has the appropriate knowledge in relation to your child's special needs.
5. **You will always be concerned about your child.** Will your child be able to make friends? Will they be able to go to school, or will their health stay stable?
6. **You will worry about them being accepted.** The world can be cruel, so you will worry whether your child will be accepted with openness.
7. **Your life won't look like other dads.** There are no playdates, after school drop-off breakfasts, or any social events if your child is overwhelmed by these activities. Depending on their condition, the exposure to so many people could even compromise their immune system.
8. **There will be a lot of medical, therapy, and hospital appointments**. Along with taking care of your child, a lot of time is spent with your child's doctors and therapists.
9. **You may often feel alone and isolated.** It may

seem like nobody understands what you are going through, and you have nobody to turn to.
10. **You may face communication difficulties.** Your child might be completely non-verbal or may have sensory issues which lead to a breakdown in communication. You must learn how to communicate what they are feeling or need.
11. **Accessibility may be difficult.** Our world isn't built to include individuals with special needs.
12. **There will be confusion.** It can be confusing to understand where your child is coming from or what they are feeling.

SURVIVAL TIPS

You are a single father to a child with special needs; hence, you will also have needs that should be looked after. I know it is not the easiest, but you need to remind yourself that if you are on the verge of a burnout, your child will be impacted because you are their sole caregiver. These are some things you will need:

1. **More Alone Time:** Where and how do you find more time for yourself? Well, it won't be easy, but it could be waking before your child or

staying up later to do something that relaxes you. If you have a trusted support group, professional help, or shared custody, make sure you take out time once a day to unwind.
2. **More Energy:** It will seem you are working overtime, and it is exhausting. Plan your day in a way that gives you short breaks. Have coffee when you feel a slump in your energy.
3. **More Money:** Please reach out to the local social services. Various agencies will have assistance programs that could help you monetarily.
4. **A Daily Routine:** A well-established daily schedule will help your child understand what to expect and lead you to lower stress.
5. **Help From Their Mother (if possible):** If the divorce was amicable and the relationship between your ex-wife and you remains cordial, convey the importance of sticking to the same routine for your child and share ideas for the betterment of your child.
6. **Therapy:** Carving a space out solely dedicated to you and what you want to speak about will be beneficial for your mental health. You can find out if your health insurance covers therapy.
7. **Family Time:** Pick a time that suits you and

your child, inform them you will be spending time differently that day, and it will be a fun filled day. You can both enjoy a break.
8. **Help and Guidance:** Build a strong support system and be okay with asking for help. Confide, reach out, and ask for help from your support group, which could be your family, friends, your Church group, or social media groups. You don't need to do everything yourself if you have a support group.

As you work toward your new normal and what it means to be a single father with a child who has special needs, remember the following.

Focus on your body and nutrition.

Try to get in physical activity during your day, even if it means going for a 20-minute jog. Exercising helps relieve stress. Focus on what goes into your body; keep it clean and organic if possible. Research indicates that parents with autistic children tend to fall sick more often and get colds, coughs, or headaches more frequently. So, take care of yourself!

Communication is key.

Learn how to interact correctly. Some children will only communicate non-verbally. Use drawings or sign language and listen with your eyes. When you show empathy and attention to your child, their stress will be reduced, and you will convey your love to them. Moreover, communicate with your child's teacher and tell them your expectations. Set up weekly or daily communication. Listen attentively to their advice and feedback about your child and their progress.

Show yourself and your child empathy.

There will be days when you will be tired, on edge, angry, or downright frustrated. This can affect your empathy towards your child, and that is okay—you are human. Show yourself the love and empathy you show your child as well. You may feel resentment toward your child sometimes and even question why you had children in the first place. Sometimes you will question if it's worth it. And that feeling is normal (even though you will feel guilty).

Know that you can't always be happy.

Your own mood will fluctuate daily because your life is so demanding. Research indicates that parents who have children with special needs face higher levels of stress and depression. You are always on the go, and it can get draining. Figure out what you are feeling, take out time for yourself, and find a way to meet your needs.

REAL LIFE EXPERIENCES OF SINGLE FATHERS

I interviewed and spoke to single fathers about how to raise a child with special needs single handedly, following is the advice and help they offered:

"If you think you had parenting nailed, then you must not have a special needs child. There was so much unlearning to do and learn all over again to meet the specific needs of my child. So, give yourself time to unlearn and learn."

- Fred W. (Cape Coral)

"Time goes by so fast that you won't even know where your day went. From sticking to a routine, to doctors' appointments, to therapy, and so on you will barely find time for yourself. But please do, even if it is waking up 10 minutes earlier than your child or sleeping 10 minutes later than your child, you will need that time for yourself."

- Billy S. (Michigan)

"Ah! The will and determination you need to get up every day can be exhausting—mentally and physically. You will always be giving and sometimes it will seem futile. But giving up isn't an option! Remember that—you've got this."

- Todd P. (Glendale)

"It was upsetting to see how my child could not do even 5% of what other 'normal' children could do. My heart ached and it still does, but it becomes a reality. If you are feeling that way, remind yourself to be in the here and now and not anticipate or worry about what is beyond your control."

- Craig L. (Pasadena)

It takes a special and kind father to raise a child with special needs. To step up to the challenge, you will have to ask for support from professional and personal connections, practice a lot of empathy, and become skilled in certain healthcare methods. In the next chapter I will cover how to discipline your children in the right manner.

8

THE RIGHT WAY TO DISCIPLINE CHILDREN AS A SINGLE DAD

The word *discipline* usually has a negative connotation—associated with punishment or yelling. But that isn't the case. Discipline also equates to good and responsible behavior and self-regulation.

Darnell faced a few issues with Darius. During the time he withdrew, he would be moody at home and snap. He also got into a fight at school. One day, Darius and Dominique got into an argument during which Darius started screaming, which was very rare for him. Darnell was very concerned, and while he did take time to sit Darius down and talk about his emotions, he also began to become more of a disciplinarian parent.

He began to ease into this new role, established himself as a disciplinarian, and began to employ various methods of discipline for his children. Of course, Darnell knew that his children would have outbursts and act up from time to time, but he became more involved and consistent in their lives. The change this caused in his children, mainly Darius, was obvious.

WHAT KIND OF FATHER ARE YOU?

It is important to understand your parenting style and then figure out if your style is impacting your child's behavior and discipline in any way. There are four basic parenting styles.

Authoritative Parenting (Just Right)

Authoritative parents are very loving and affectionate, and they offer a sense of structure in their child's life. This type of parent gives reasonable demands and sets consistent limits. They express warmth and affection and listen to their child's point of view. For instance, if their child wants to stay up past their bedtime, instead of saying no, the parents suggest talking about it. They ask why and listen to their child's response. After giving their own concerns, the parent and child come to a compromise. Such parents usually set rules and encourage the child to follow these rules for their betterment. Authoritative parents do not use power to gain anything from the child.

Such parents offer guidance in a rationalized manner which leads to effective communication between the child and the parent. Authoritative parenting is the best style of parenting because it leads to children being emotionally healthy. Children who grow up with authoritative parents are self-assured, great in school, have great social skills, are less involved in alcohol, have good self-esteem, and display better coping strategies.

Authoritarian Parenting (Too Hard)

Authoritarianism is more about conformity and obedience. It sticks to the orthodox narrative of, "I am the adult, and you are the child." There is no discussion, and it is a very strict relationship. Authoritarian parents wish to shape the behavior and personality of their child according to a certain standard, and if these standards are not met, they are punished. Usually, there is no logic or rationale behind these set standards. Such parents have high demands from their children, are less engaged, do not encourage open communication, and expect their children to be extremely obedient.

If the scenario about bedtime is adapted to this style of parenting, the parent would say "no" without any hesitation, and there would be no room for negotiation. Children who have authoritarian parents usually turn out to be anxious, withdrawn, and unhappy. They have lower self-confidence and poor coping mechanisms.

They also lack self-discipline, are associated with poor academic behavior, have unprotected sex, and suffer from substance abuse. Moreover, such children are more dependent on parental guidance since they lack self-confidence.

Permissive Parenting

In permissive parenting, children run the show, and anything goes. The parent makes few demands and rarely uses punishment. They try to play the role of friend rather than a parent. Such parents tend to behave in a very affirmative manner and avoid conflict. Furthermore, permissive parents escape any behavioral control, shirk away from establishing rules, and have fewer expectations from their children. Such parents give the space to their children to partake in activities without thinking about repercussions. Because such parents demand next to nothing from their children and are more indulgent, their children turn out lacking self-discipline. Moreover, the children of permissive parents are unhappy and lack the skill of self-regulation. They also do not do well in school and do not respond well to authority.

Uninvolved Parents

These parents are uninvolved and indifferent to their child's needs, especially emotional needs. These parents are stricter, and they even tend to be neglectful at times. This type of parenting only focuses on filling the child's basic needs such as being fed, drinking water, and providing shelter. This is also termed as rejecting and neglecting parenting. Such parents usually struggle with substance abuse or are overly involved in careers with no time for their child or family. Uninvolved parenting leads to emotionally withdrawn, fearful, and anxious individuals. Such children are also more at risk of substance abuse. They have low self-esteem and low self-confidence. They do not fare well in school.

WHAT NOT TO DO

I understand that there is a lot going on in your life. As a single father, you will be overwhelmed, on edge, or snappy, so you could fall into unhealthy and toxic disciplining behaviors with your child. Let's start with what you shouldn't be doing as a single father in terms of discipline.

- Don't lose your temper. There will be moments when you will see red, and all you want to do is scream or shout, but please refrain from disciplining your child when you are angry. Raising your voice or losing your temper sets a bad example for your child, and they may start

to believe that anger and violence is the acceptable way of dealing and discipline.
- Don't give physical punishment. Spanking or lightly jerking your child is a big no-no! It will make your child feel that physical punishment is the way to deal with conflict and anger.
- Don't be inconsistent. Don't laugh at your child's misbehavior and then chastise it the next time. Keep your responses the same for any misbehavior.
- Don't use bribery. If you try to bribe your child with a reward to behave a certain way, they will begin to misbehave to get the reward.
- Don't use guilt. Don't use ingratiation as a method to get your child to listen to you.
- Don't constantly lecture. Telling them a long story of why they shouldn't be misbehaving rarely results in learning.
- Don't compare. Comparison between siblings or friends leads to resentment.

DISCIPLINING MISTAKES DIVORCED PARENTS MAKE

In shared custody, disciplining between two divorced parents can get difficult. It can be challenging for you, your ex-partner, and your child. There are some common mistakes that divorced parents make while disciplining their child, such as:

- **Trying to the be the Favorite:** You might be tempted to be the cooler or more fun parent by bending certain rules, but this will surely backfire. Your child will end up comparing you and turn it into a contest which doesn't work in anyone's favor.
- **Being Untruthful About Behavior:** You may tell your ex-partner how your child is perfectly well-behaved at your house and question why they act out in their house. Be honest about your child's behavior because it will be vital in taking consistent and joint steps towards disciplining your child.
- **Badmouthing the Mother:** You may not have the best relationship with your ex-partner, but she is still your child's mother. Don't try to mold your child's mind by sharing negative opinions about their mother.
- **Feeling Sorry:** Being lenient or pitying your child because they are feeling the brunt of the divorce is okay sometimes, but it shouldn't be a consistent pattern. This can lead to your child harboring a victim mentality, which is unhealthy.

- **Overcompensation:** If your child's mother is extremely strict, you might want to be easy-going; however, be mindful that you cannot compensate for your ex-partners behavior. That is between your child and their mother.

WHAT TO DO

Finally, we are at the point where I can share disciplining techniques with you. There are various methods and techniques.

- Do reward good behavior. Make sure to compliment, reward and recognize your child's good behavior—they will try to do it more often when they feel validated for it.
- Do explain natural and logical consequences. Sometimes your child will do something, and you don't have to lecture them. Instead, you let them sit with the natural outcome of their action. For instance, if they break their toy, the natural consequence is that they will not have a toy to play with.
- Do rescind privileges. While taking away a privilege, see that the privilege is related to their behavior, of value to your child, and taken away in a timely manner.

- Do use the timeout technique. If you want a break from your child's behavior or if you know exactly what they did wrong, then use the timeout technique. Make sure the timeout place is boring and quiet. Do not use the bathroom, their bedroom, or any outdoor space for this technique.
- Do be consistent. Habits are formed by repetition and consistency. Do not give in during a timeout or bend the rules because your child is getting angry with you, stick to your rules.
- Do communicate the discipline plan. Tell your child what you are doing and why you are doing it if they are old enough to understand.
- Do respect your child. Your child is an individual with self-esteem, hence show them respect even while you discipline them.
- Do see what is appropriate for your child's development. Before disciplining your child, see that your child understands what you are asking of them. Most times children cannot comprehend what you are asking of them.
- Do listen to their side of the story. Give them space to relate their side of the story or the reason for their misbehavior. Understanding where they are coming from

can help you understand the reason behind their action.
- Do pick your battles. Don't make everything into a big deal. Give the appropriate energy required for the issue, otherwise you will always be disciplining and exhausted.
- Do give unconditional love. Even when your child has done something you disagree with, they need to know you love them but are angry or disappointed with them.

AGE BY AGE GUIDE

Toddlers

I'll start with toddlers who fall in the age bracket between 1 to 3-years-old. With toddlers, you will observe tantrums because they cannot explicitly express what they do and do not want. You can practice the following disciplining techniques:

- Toddlers are beginning to build their independence, so try to give them some control over the choices they can make. For example, ask them if they want to brush their teeth first or change into their PJs first.
- Try to keep your cool because reactions, whether positive or negative, will give your

child the attention they thrive on. If they toss the contents of their plate on the floor, calmly explain that they shouldn't be throwing food on the floor. Keep it simple and short.
- Shut down tantrums before they blow up. Figure out what triggers their tantrums and prepare beforehand.
- Timeouts work out great once your child turns two. Take your toddler to a different room where they can think about what they have done. Keep the timeout equivalent to the age of your child.

Pre-schoolers

Pre-schoolers fall within the age bracket of 3 to 5-years-old. By this age, your child's memory and communication will begin developing. You will observe whining and not listening from their end. You can practice the following disciplining techniques:

- Never ask them more than once. For instance, ask them nicely and calmly to put their toys away. If they don't listen, tell them a negative outcome, say you will count to 5 and if the toys aren't put away, you will not get to play with them tomorrow.
- Encourage their good behavior and validate it.

- Act the way you want them to behave. Children learn a lot from your actions.

School-aged Children

School-aged children fall in the age bracket of 5 to 10-years-old. By this age, your child will be better able to express feelings and practice self-control. You will observe compliance issues. You can practice the following disciplining techniques:

- Become their coach by phrasing questions like a coach. Help your child learn from their mistakes and ask them how they can do things differently next time.
- Give second chances and thank them when they behave appropriately the next time.

Tweens

Tweens fall in the age bracket of 10 to 12-years-old. By this age, your child is more independent and more social. You will observe a power struggle between the two of you, back talk, and crankiness. You can practice the following disciplining techniques:

- Try not to dictate your rules to them. Offer flexibility which garners co-operation.

- Negotiate at a better time. Try not to negotiate with them when they're cranky; rather, be firm when they are cranky and negotiate when they are calmer.
- Apply the "when and then" technique. This sets a boundary for the child.
- Be clear about your expectations and don't waver from them. For instance, if your child is rude, tell them you expect respect and will be spoken to politely.

Teens

Teens fall in the age category of 13 to 19-years old. Their bodies are changing, there is a change in hormonal levels, and they are seeking independence. You will observe a major attitude issue. You can practice the following disciplining techniques:

- Try to stay calm. Nothing good comes out of two warring factions.
- Set appropriate limits and boundaries.

GET THOSE CHORES DONE

When your child is old enough and you can delegate chores to them, please do. However, if you feel they are wavering from their responsibilities, engage in the following disciplining method:

- Make a list of chores that need to be done by everyone.
- Set a timeline for the chore to be completed.
- Establish a system of chores, what counts as the chore being complete, and how many reminders will be given.
- Make it known that there will be no iPad or going out with friends until chores are complete.
- Post the chore chart around the house.

This will help set rules and limits in relation to chores for everyone in the house.

REAL LIFE EXPERIENCES OF SINGLE FATHERS

I interviewed and spoke to single fathers about how to raise a son single handedly. Following is the advice and help they offered:

"Consistency and calmness are the key to disciplining your child as a single father. You will be at your wits end if you don't keep your calm."

- Earl J. (Harrisburg)

"Never engage in physical punishment when you discipline your child. You don't want them to fear you. When they fear you, they will resent you. So, look into other ways of conveying your message and be mindful of your anger."

- Terrence G. (Cedar Falls)

"When you are angry at your child, they may think you don't love them anymore and may feel rejected. I know it is hard to tell your child that you love them when you are angry or disappointed in them, but try to convey that message so they don't feel you have stopped loving them—that's a lonely place for your child to be in."

- Gilbert F. (Newport)

Even celebrity fathers have shared their experiences of disciplining their children.

"I'm a softie, but I'm also strict. It's probably confusing for Jack. I'm probably the strict parent, but also pretty loving and affectionate as well. I think you've got to get respect, do what you say you're going to do, and make your kids toe the line and all that stuff. But at the same time, you give them lots of hugs and kisses."

- Chris Pratt (*Slice*, 2021)

"I think the most important thing is to always be involved in every aspect of their life. To give them enough trust that they can share things with you. I don't want them to be terrified of me, you know? But I don't want them to think they can do whatever they want and get away with it, either, because they can't."

- Mark Wahlberg (*Slice*, 2021)

One of the most misjudged and discussed parts of single parenthood is discipline. It's often associated with making your child suffer for their behavior. But you know better now, and you understand that the correct guidance and nurturing can help them behave well and responsibly. In the next chapter, I will discuss the single father guide to dating.

9

A NEW MOM FOR THE KIDS?

When Darnell eventually began dating someone new, all hell broke loose in the house. Dominique and Darius did not respond well to their father finding a partner for himself. The conflict led to Darnell ending his relationship. However, he wasn't happy about doing that. I asked him to sit down with his children and talk to them about what they were feeling and what their fears were regarding someone new in their lives.

At first, he was met with a lot of resistance, reluctance, mood swings, nods and grunts. But his children finally warmed up to the idea of having a conversation, which proved beneficial for everyone. He heard his children out. He realized how he had rushed into a relationship without telling his children and assured them that his new partner was not going to take their mother's place.

Eventually, he got back with his partner, and they have been together ever since. Through dealing with the matter in a correct manner, it is possible to allow yourself to date, fall in love, and even re-marry. You deserve a second chance at happiness.

DATING

This is an entirely new scenario for you. You now have children and more responsibilities, so you may be telling yourself dating is not worth the time and effort. Maybe you fear getting into a relationship and getting hurt, but you deserve love and companionship in your life. Ask yourself the following questions before you begin dating again, and please answer them honestly.

- Am I ready to date?
- Do I have the time for dates?
- What am I looking for on a date? What am I supposed to be looking for?
- Will I let my date meet my children?
- Am I truly over my ex?

Tips

When you answer these questions, and you decide that you are ready to entertain the idea of dating, here are some tips to follow.

- **Timing:** Do not rush into the next relationship. Give yourself time to process your previous relationship and time to heal. When you think you are in a good position, then consider getting back into the dating circuit.
- **Honesty:** You will have to tell your date about your children and if you have lost your partner or are divorced. This is a part of your life, but beyond this, you don't have to go into detail unless this becomes a long-term relationship.
- **Parent First, Partner Second:** Dating won't be the same as when you did not have children. You won't be able to chat for hours on end on the phone or meet them for hours. Your time will be divided with your children. Remember your priorities and take it slow.
- **Expectations:** Know what you want and what you are looking for before dating again. Are you looking to have a good time, a long-term relationship, or just wanting to speak to someone? Being clear about what you want will make it easier to convey it to your date. Don't

expect your children to be overjoyed about you dating but don't let that throw you off from dating. Keep your expectations realistic.
- **Protection:** If you and your date are having sex, do use protection.
- **Honesty:** This is entirely up to you! Gauge your relationship, the openness, and the timing and tell your children whenever you think is the right time. Do be mindful of telling them when you're dating and when you're looking for a long-term relationship.
- **Sleeping Over:** As your relationship progresses, you might want your partner to stay the night. Take into consideration what your children will say and think and if they will be comfortable with the idea. Keep your expectations realistic.
- **Safety:** Please consider your family's safety and privacy and don't share too much personal information too soon.

The Other Perspective

While you are thinking about dating again, do take into consideration what the other side may feel or assume about you as a single father. I'll break it into the pros and cons:

Pros

- He wants to settle down and not play games.
- He will be sensitive and nurturing because he is a father.
- He will love me for who I am rather than what I look like.
- If he is a father to a daughter, he will be more empathetic toward me.

Cons

- There will be mama drama with his ex-partner.
- His children will be his top priority, not me.
- He won't have a lot of money to spend on me.
- I will not be welcomed very warmly into his life by his children.

HOW TO HAVE THE DATING CONVERSATION WITH YOUR CHILD

Now that I have given you tips on how to get back into the dating game, let's move on to the next step—telling your children.

Beforehand, you need to examine what your relationship with your partner is. If you are truly committed to your date, then consider having your children meet your partner. Don't rush your child; it leaves them feeling vulnerable and triggers their attachment fears. Moreover, ask yourself whether you see yourself with your partner in the future. Can they fit into your family? If the answers are yes, then go ahead and introduce your partner to your children. Before you do introduce your partner, make sure to do the following:

- Have a dialogue with your children.
- Calm their fear of abandonment and any other fear that comes up.
- Show them your commitment to them.
- Share your happiness and excitement for your partner with them.
- Make it clear you aren't looking for their approval and neither are you giving them an ultimatum.
- Let them know you love them, and they are your priority.
- Ask them how they feel and be open to what they have to say.

If all goes well, you can move on to scheduling a meeting with your child and your partner. Remember:

- Make it casual and relaxed.
- Be yourself.

- Have a family friendly activity.
- Do something fun.
- Don't expect too much.

Take your time my friend! There is no rush, just remember you cannot control anybody's reactions, so keep it real!

GET GOING

Time to put all this advice into action. Don't expect someone great to fall out of the sky. You will have to be proactive. Dating has changed since the last time you went on your first date. Technology has made it easier to find a match. Look into your options. What do you prefer? Consider your time, how much effort you can put in, the amount of energy, and your age and see which option is the most suited to you regarding meeting someone new. Some options to consider are:

- Online dating (There are numerous websites, such as Tinder, Bumble, First Met, Our Time, and Single Parent Love.)
- Ask a friend to introduce you to someone
- Believe in luck (If you have the patience and believe in kismet, you may bump into the next

love of your life at the grocery store or the gym.)
- Alumni events (Maybe you rekindle a spark with your high school sweetheart.)

Whatever you choose, be patient. Nothing materializes overnight. Do not be in a hurry to find the next love of your life; take it slow and enjoy the process.

REAL LIFE EXPERIENCES OF SINGLE FATHERS

I interviewed and spoke to single fathers about dating again. This is the advice they had to offer:

"Be honest from the get-go. You need to know who is in for the real deal—you being a father, having a job, looking after the house and dating as well. If they feel you don't match what they're looking for, it's better to exit earlier rather than later."

- Jacob C. (Pittsburg)

"I didn't think dating was worth it, I didn't have time for another commitment in my life. But once my child started high school, I got lonely because I had so much spare time. So, I began dating again. Don't wait for loneliness to creep in, if you feel you're ready, just go for it."

- Seth A. (Ann Arbor)

"I used to think I was being unfair to my children when I would consider getting remarried. There was a sense of guilt, but I realized I have to do it for myself, I deserve happiness and love again! Remind yourself of that."

- Wade J. (Austin)

"Oh man, the number of dates who have ghosted me after finding out I am a single father are one too many! But don't be discouraged, it never was easy to find the right person, so keep at it and soon you will be with someone you are truly happy with."

- Shawn M. (Florida)

Unless you are completely uninterested in romantic attachments, chances are that you will look into dating again. When you do, don't ignore your child's needs and emotions. Having a "new woman" in their lives is a big deal, and the last thing you want to do is underestimate the effect of this on them. In the next and final chapter, I will talk about how to make it through the rough times.

10

STRATEGIES FOR THE TOUGH TIMES

Darnell's struggle seemed never ending. His life was marked with grief, stress, depression, and anxiety. While he was mourning his wife, he had to be there for his children, manage the house and expenses, overlook his children's academics, manage his job—the list was never ending.

This took a toll on him. There were moments I would find him crying in his room, and there were times when he would be on the verge of physically collapsing because he had so much on his plate. One thing that struck me the most was how he once told me, "Alfie, I don't even have time to be sad, and when I do get time to be sad, I can't handle it and it breaks me." He kept himself so busy that he experienced burnout often, but he realized how this was affecting his entire life, his family, his office, and so on.

Darnell did eventually turn his life around with adequate family support, self-help, therapy, and just slowing down to allow himself to feel. The change had a positive effect on everyone. I wanted to share his experience, so you know you aren't alone. Others struggle just like you, it is a part of life. But you can make it through this!

ON THE VERGE OF A BREAKDOWN?

It is not easy, and I don't want to sugarcoat it for you. There will be various stressors and triggers in your life:

There is too much going on.

Stressor: There is one person doing everything, and that person is you! While you are caught up in the day-to-day routine, stress and exhaustion keep building up which is unhealthy because then anything can trigger you and you can have a breakdown.

Solution: When you begin to feel overwhelmed, overworked, irritable, and snappy (you will), give yourself time to step back. Engage in an activity you like, do something that relaxes you, and then step back into your life. It could be anything from going for a walk, a jog, a coffee, reading a book, exercising, and so on.

You are the sole financial supporter.

Stressor: All the financial responsibility falls on you as well, which to be honest, can be scary and stressful. This can also be a trigger for stress and anxiety attacks. Childcare, groceries, utilities, and rent are where most of your money will end up going, but there are also emergency costs. You're always wondering whether you will ever have enough money.

Solution: You will keep worrying if you don't start budgeting and saving. As I have mentioned before in chapter 4, seek out government assistance and support. There is no shame in seeking help. You don't have to do everything alone; that will just add more stress.

Co-parenting conflicts are inevitable.

Stressor: If you don't get along with your ex-partner, co-parenting can become challenging and stressful. If you are already overworked, you will be easily triggered which can lead to angry confrontation.

Solution: What you can focus on is keeping your parenting relationship separate from your personal relationship with your ex-partner. Be mindful that your child and their happiness is the priority and agree on a parenting plan that works for both of you. Make sure the parenting plan covers finances, routines, and schedules. Moreover, understand and accept that your ex-partner will have a role in your child's life—whether you like it or not.

You need time for yourself.

Stressor: You will constantly be putting your children's needs ahead of yours, which leads to no time for yourself. Parenting is rife with sacrifices, but that doesn't mean you neglect yourself entirely. Single parents feel a lot of guilt for taking out time for themselves. Know that this is not a simple want, it is essential need for a healthy functioning life. And while it may seem impossible to take out time, it isn't. You control your time. If you keep giving while staying empty yourself, you will be unhappy and resentful.

Solution: Turn to your support system, your family, and friends. Ask for help and carve time out for yourself. Moreover, learn to delegate if your children are old enough.

It is lonely.

Stressor: While you will be missing the romantic aspect in your life, you will also feel the burden of making decisions alone, which can be taxing. You won't be able to share ideas and face challenges that can be upsetting.

Solution: Just remember that you don't exist in isolation. You have a support group in your family and friends, so reach out to them. Don't just limit yourself to them. Become friends with other single fathers and mothers and join a single parent support group. Knowing you are a part of something bigger will reassure you that you are not alone.

DEPRESSION & LONELINESS IN SINGLE FATHERS

Depression doesn't come suddenly; it comes in slow motions. It seeps into your daily life and your thought process, and you don't even realize it until it takes a complete toll on you. There will be days when you just want to cry, scream, or shut yourself alone in a room. Depression can take on a lot of forms: irritability, loss of appetite, difficulty sleeping, withdrawal from social life, constant sadness, suicidal thoughts, and low energy.

You will try to be strong and keep a brave face for your child, but you are allowed to be sad. However, know when to step out of that negative cycle when you're going in too deep. Maybe it seems to keep you in a downward spiral, your mind seems like a dark place to be, and all you want to do is escape it. Moreover, you have a child to take care of, so you feel you cannot afford to be depressed. So, you put aside your feelings and just focus on your child. You push your depression back into the deepest crevice of your mind, but it is still there, lingering and feeling heavy. You feel lonely and isolated.

It is statistically proven that single parents feel more stressed and depressed. The first thing to do when you feel any of this is to recognize and accept it. Denying won't do you any good! Recognition and acceptance are the first steps toward making a change in your life.

Then, begin therapy, even though it will feel daunting and tiring. Incorporate exercise, even if it is a 15-minute walk. Reach out to your support group and allow them into your life. Take out time for yourself to do self-care. Ignore the unkind, dark voices inside that whisper you don't deserve to feel good or that you will fail. Tell yourself you are doing your best and it takes time.

There is a strong sense of loneliness as a single father. Ask yourself when you feel the loneliest and how you can overcome that loneliness. Try getting involved in communal activities, become involved in your child's school parent groups, and reach out to your support group. Get in touch with old friends and try to stay in touch with them. We don't realize this, but social connections are important in our life. Meet your family or friends for coffee, a drink, or lunch once a week. When you have people in your life, those who love you and care for you, they will reach out to you. When you begin scheduling meetups, you will have something to look forward to, and you will feel less lonely. I want to make it clear that you are not alone and that you can come out of the dark place and into a happy and lighter place. Life is filled with ups and downs. Life will push you to the ground, but we must stand up again!

MINDFULNESS

It is common to get caught up with stress and anxiety, worry about our children, be overwhelmed, be upset, and have difficulty coping with loss and guilt. When all this seems to be on your plate, it can be daunting, so I want to suggest practicing mindfulness in such times.

For You

What exactly is mindfulness? It is the ability to be present in the here and now. It means being aware of our emotions, feelings, and environment and being empathic. Being mindful can help us remain calm in triggering and stressful situations. How can you practice mindfulness for yourself? Here's a list of suggestions:

1. Build a strong support system to seek help from, speak to, and fall back on.
2. Be responsible with your finances—save, budget, and organize your expenses.
3. Have a healthy and consistent routine that works for you and your family.
4. Keep things simple and be okay with that.
5. Take out quality time for your children.
6. Take out time for yourself and your needs.
7. Practice consistency in all that you do.
8. Be honest with yourself and your child.
9. Don't feel shy or guilty asking for help.
10. Be kind to yourself.
11. Don't fight the negatives; accept them and work with them.
12. Be okay with everything not being perfect.
13. Stay positive.

For the Family

While mindfulness is important for you, it is also important to instill in your children. They can benefit from it. Whatever helps your children tune into their feelings will help with mindfulness. There are various ways you can teach them this skill

Counting Breaths: The technique is to breathe in and out slowly while counting each breath. When you feel your mind start to wander, start from the beginning. Make a game out of it so your child can enjoy it. This breathing technique also helps with sleeping at night.

Mindful Eating: Most times we eat mindlessly. Just like the breathing technique which grounds us, eating mindfully also has benefits, such as not overeating and good digestion. When you become mindful of what you eat, you eat less and enjoy the food. First, bring your child's awareness to how hungry they are, and while they eat, ask them to describe what they are feeling. Ask them to identify shapes, sounds, texture, smell, and taste.

Mindful Coloring: Coloring is akin to meditation. Mindful coloring requires you to keep out thoughts and put your energy toward coloring. Since you must stay within lines, choose colors, and focus on angles, you will be zoned into one activity.

Mindful listening: This is best practiced when your child is relaxed. You can ask them to tune into the sounds of the environment. Listen for animal sounds, human sounds, and motorized sounds. If you want to practice the same with music, ask them to identify the instrument they can hear, different melodies, and sounds.

Body scan: This is used to focus awareness on our body and the sensations we feel. Ask your child to lie on their back and close their eyes. Then, ask them to squeeze their muscles very tight and hold that position for a few seconds and then ask them to relax. Ask them to notice the different sensations they feel.

Feel Your Heartbeat: Ask your child to jump up and down until their heartbeat accelerates. Then tell them to be still and place their hand over their heart, close their eyes, and feel the heartbeat slow down. This technique also helps children calm down.

Weather Reporting: Ask your child what they are feeling by associating it with the weather. For instance, you can describe feeling grey and gloomy or bright and sunny. They will then view their feelings as something natural, and it will be relatable for them.

Stare at the Clouds: This one is simple. Just lie on your back to look up at the clouds passing by. It really slows you down and makes you be present in the moment. This also helps with their imagination.

REAL LIFE EXPERIENCES FROM SINGLE FATHERS

I interviewed and spoke to single fathers about depression, loneliness, and mindfulness. This is what they had to say:

"I would feel guilty about being depressed and would shove it aside thinking I was doing everyone a favor, except I wasn't! I was doing a disservice to myself. It took an emotional breakdown in front of my 13-year-old son to realize I had to accept my depression and process it. So please don't run away from what you're feeling."

- Joseph B. (Minneapolis)

"When I first heard about mindfulness, my reaction was 'what?' I thought it was a whole load of nonsense. But my therapist used it a lot to bring awareness to my mind and body. It helped me focus on the situation at hand rather than worrying about the future."

- Michael S. (Arkansas)

"It was lonely for the first two years after my ex-wife left me. It was just my daughter and me. There were days when she would be the only other human I would have a conversation with. I didn't even realize how much I craved adult connec-

tions till I began going out again. It took time, but I got there, I got to the point where I put the comfort of loneliness away."

- LeBron M. (Utah)

"The expectations I set on myself as a single father were unrealistic. I would set goals which were unattainable. But I soon realized that perfection wasn't going to work out, I just had to do what I thought was good enough and be happy with that."

- Samuel P. (Houston)

The stress that accompanies single fatherhood can affect any man. However, through caring for yourself, your well-being, your family connections, and practices such as meditation and mindfulness, you can begin to work with the new responsibilities and demands in your life in a composed manner.

YOU ARE A SUPERHERO!

You have made it to the end of the book! Taking out time to read the entire book is a sign of self-care because you made time to learn something new for yourself.

I want to take this chance to tell you that I am proud of you; I admire your courage and strength. It takes a lot to give love, kindness, and care to your children while also running a house, managing a job, earning money, doing chores, and so on. You are filled with love and affection for everyone, and I hope you can give the same love and affection to yourself. I know it is not the easiest journey for you, but here you are, with your family—hopefully in good health!

There's something you can do to make single fatherhood work better. Be it creating a budget for next month, explaining bodily changes to your adolescent daughter, teaching your son how to tie a knot, or reaching out to social support groups, just go for it.

Throughout this book, I have covered certain topics in detail to make it easier for you to understand, cope, and progress in your journey as a single father. You can do all the following tasks:

- Help your child cope with the loss of their mother.
- Manage and organize time and your life.
- Manage your finances better.
- Raise your daughter.
- Raise your son.
- Raise your child with special needs.
- Discipline your children.
- Begin dating again.
- Be mindful.
- Cope with struggles and stress.

It is time for you to put all that you have learned into action and make the changes you think are going to benefit you.

I want to make a list of statements which you can tell yourself from time to time whenever you feel overwhelmed. Use these statements to give validation to yourself.

- I have got this!
- I can get through this!
- It is okay I am that I am feeling sad, I'll give myself time.
- I need to take out time for myself.
- What is stressing me out right now and how can I ease it?
- It's okay to draw boundaries and say no!
- Today is hard for me, so I won't be hard on myself.

I wish you the best of luck in your life as a single father.

BIBLIOGRAPHY

Bureau, U. C. (n.d.). *Fathers in the United States*. Census.-Gov. https://www.census.gov/programs-surveys/sis/resources/news/fathers.html

Campbell, D., & editor, D. C. H. policy. (2019, January 17). Parents' break-up more likely to harm mental health of children aged seven to 14. *The Guardian*. https://www.theguardian.com/society/2019/jan/17/parents-break-up-more-likely-to-harm-mental-health-of-children-aged-seven-to-14

D'Onofrio, B., & Emery, R. (2019). Parental divorce or separation and children's mental health. *World Psychiatry, 18*(1), 100–101. https://doi.org/10.1002/wps.20590

McQuillan, M. E., Bates, J. E., Staples, A. D., & Deater Deckard, K. (2019). Maternal stress, sleep, and parenting. *Journal of Family Psychology: JFP: Journal of the Division of Family Psychology of the American Psychological Association (Division 43), 33*(3), 349–359. https://doi.org/10.1037/fam0000516

Parenting worksheets (Assessment tool). (2016, July 3). *Free Social Work Tools and Resources: SocialWorkersToolbox.Com.* http://www.socialworkerstoolbox.com/parenting-worksheets-assessment-tool/

Stack, R. J., & Meredith, A. (2018). The impact of financial hardship on single parents: An exploration of the journey from social distress to seeking help. *Journal of Family and Economic Issues, 39*(2), 233–242. https://doi.org/10.1007/s10834-017-9551-6

Zuckerman, A. (2020, May 26). *61 SINGLE PARENT STATISTICS: 2020/2021 OVERVIEW, DEMOGRAPHICS & FACTS.* Compare Camp. https://comparecamp.com/single-parent-statistics/

QUICK NOTE

Positive reviews from awesome customers like you help others to feel confident about choosing this book too. Could you take 60 seconds on Amazon or any platform where you got the book and share your happy experiences? There are other awesome books like *The First Time Father, The First Time Father: Baby's First Year, Sleep Training like a Pro, Single Dad Parenting like a Pro, Potty Training Like a Pro, Discipline Like a Pro, All Fathers Memorable Jokes* and others still to come. Any ideas you would like Alfie Thomas to write about or improve on, his email is always open. You can reach out to:

books@alfie-thomas.com and

https://thealfiethomas.com/

https://mirabellen.activehosted.com/f/1,

https://www.facebook.com/groups/1253933881690907, and

https://www.instagram.com/alfiethomas.official/

We will be forever grateful. Thank you in advance for helping us out.

www.ingramcontent.com/pod-product-compliance
Lightning Source LLC
Chambersburg PA
CBHW042125100526
44587CB00026B/4180